Common Sense II

Common Sense II

A Remedy For The Current American Crisis

NORMAN R. MANCUSO, PHD

ISBN 061563284X
ISBN 978-0615632841

Manufactured in the United States of America.

Published by NRM Books
24 Terrane Avenue

Natick, MA 01760

Library of Congress Control Number: 2012907333
NRM Books, Natick, MA

Dedication

To my sisters, Theresa Marie and Carolina,
Who suffers from early-onset Alzheimer's disease,
And to my loving children, Diane, Lisa, and John,
This work is dedicated.

Epigraph

"When it shall be said in any country in the world my poor are happy; neither ignorance nor distress is to be found among them; my jails are empty of prisoners, my streets of beggars; the aged are not in want; the taxes are not oppressive; the rational world is my friend, because I am a friend of its happiness: When these things can be said, there may that country boast of its Constitution and its Government."

Thomas Paine

Acknowledgements

I would like to thank those individuals who in many ways are responsible for the success of this book. To my sister, Theresa Marie Mancuso, whose comments and suggestions were only outdone by the professionalism and artistry with which she produced the cover design. To my children, Diane Czebieniak, Lisa Mancuso and John Mancuso, each of whom read the manuscript and offered suggestions for its improvement, in addition to offering encouragement when the task seemed insurmountable. To anyone whom I may have forgotten, I can only say that's something I do every day and no one is sorrier than I am! Naturally, any errors are my own.

Table of Contents

Table of Contents

List of Figure & Tables

Apologia

"When men yield up the privilege of thinking, the last shadow of liberty quits the horizon."

Thomas Paine

On January 10, 1776, Thomas Paine published his seminal work entitled *Common Sense*.[1] Within three months of its publication, well over 100,000 copies had been sold. *Common Sense* arrived at a crisis point in American history, pointing the way to the soon-to-be-inevitable revolutionary war, for within six months the Declaration of Independence would be signed. This, as we all know, ultimately resulted in the birth of The United States of America, ready and willing to take its place among the nations of the world. Although this would not occur for several years hence, the pamphlet enabled many of the citizens of the new country to realize the stakes before it and to resolve to do their utmost to support the foundation of the fledgling country.

America will, I hope, forgive me for usurping the title of Paine's masterful work. I believe that we are on the cusp of another great crisis in the history of this wonderful country. Indeed, if we should continue upon the course which is currently set, the United States of America, as we know it, will cease to exist. We will have sold our heritage, and that of our children and grandchildren and their heirs forever. This has resulted from our failure to live both within our means and according to the two unparalleled documents which gave our country its birth. America has long been a beacon of hope to many in the world, oppressed in one way or another, and who have longed to join us. It has been our destiny to hold this beacon proudly before the world. Now we have reached a point in our history where we have allowed this beacon to become considerably tarnished.

It is true that many in the world do not see democracy as we see it. We have made many mistakes, as we freely admit. Nevertheless, in spite of our faults, people from all countries of the world still seek to immigrate to the United States of America. We remain that beacon to the rest of the world, tarnished or not. It is time for us to address these faults, and once more, to burnish this beacon to blinding brilliance. In doing so, let us remember and espouse the following words:

"The cause of America is, in a great measure, the cause of all mankind."

Thomas Paine

Prologue

"Those who expect to reap the blessings of freedom, must, like men, undergo the fatigues of supporting it."

Thomas Paine

America exists in a state not unlike the beleaguered union between a husband and a wife, wherein change on both sides is warranted. Make no mistake about it, while America is in need of some change, the other party, namely, the American citizens, is likewise in need of a great degree of change. In other words, we can blame the current state of the union on others who have clearly led us down the garden path. Equally to blame are the citizens who seem to have done nothing less than to aid and abet the course taken by misguided political leaders, who have forgotten that they are the servants, not only of the people, but of the Constitution as well.

When asked by a woman what type of government we had achieved, the venerable Benjamin Franklin replied *"A republic, if you can keep it"*.[2] Therefore, we can take it on good authority, that the keeping of this Republic is more the responsibility of the citizen, than it is of the politicians who guide it. This does not sit well with many who would rather stand by and judge the political leaders of whichever party they are not aligned with. Nevertheless it would seem clear at this point that America indeed has problems. As the cartoon character Pogo said *"We have met the enemy and they are us"*.

Clearly then, we have two tasks at hand, the first of which is to fix our own problems before we attempt to fix those of the government. Like any good counselor, it is incumbent upon us to recognize that there are faults on the part of both parties. To recognize only those of one side of the altercation would no doubt cause the other party to accuse us of acting unfairly.

Before we go any further on this particular issue, we should try to retrace the steps which have led us to this position. If one is to look carefully through the Constitution of the United States of America, one will not find any reference to the existence of a privileged class. Nevertheless, we do indeed have a privileged class among us. That class is none other than the legislators who hold elected office in either the Senate or the House of Representatives. However, they are not alone, as the same issue applies to other office-holders in the remaining branches of government, both State and Federal. One needs only to go to the Internet and look up the salaries and other privileges of members of the House and Senate[3] to see that their salary is approximately 3.4 times that of the average American worker! Currently, Senators and Representatives are paid $174,000.

They also have other extensive privileges, not the least of which is healthcare benefits which far exceed those which they are willing to grant to the average American. Consider the recently passed healthcare law, officially called The Patient Protection and Affordable Care Act (PPACA) and commonly known as "ObamaCare".[4] Few, if any, of these legislators had even read this bill (which is estimated to be some 2500 pages in length.) before passing it. In spite of this appalling lack of knowledge, they were astute enough to exempt themselves from its mandates. This is just the tip of the iceberg. In fact, U.S. Senators and Congressmen are one of a group of the most highly paid politicians anywhere in the world. Indeed, they even have the ability to raise their own salaries. The real cream is that they are capable of passing laws which affect and benefit only a small group of people in the country. Because of this, the probability exists that they will be rewarded by these same people. Often this takes place in the form of one or more amendments to a pending bill. Most of their colleagues have no interest in these amendment(s), but may wish to see the bill passed. They vote in favor, in part, in order to avail themselves of this same shady practice at a later date. Most say or do nothing about this selfish miscarriage of justice.

Their knowledge also puts them in a position to benefit from insider trading and other stock deals. To be sure, not all of them are guilty of these things. Nonetheless, in the words of my father, *"Opportunity makes the thief."* It is clear that something must be done to prevent these situations from being abused. In fact, it must be said that, perhaps in an effort to "clean up their act" prior to the impending election, laws have recently been passed to prevent this insider trading.[5] However, these are not the only problems which face our country.

There are others which are addressed in the chapters which follow, all of which are of sufficient danger to eventually cause the destruction of the country we hold so dear. It seems clear that the problem of illegal immigration would not exist if it were not for the fact that living in this country was not widely understood to be the most desirable place in the world in which to live. People have been immigrating to this country since its very beginning. That is easy to understand because at that time there was no other country in the world where so many freedoms were so abundant. This will not continue to be so unless we take a firm stand and protect those freedoms that we all cherish.

In the final analysis, only we can prevent America from being destroyed. It can only be destroyed from within, by people who are unwilling to pass along to the next generations, that which they received intact from their parents and forebears. It is up to us to make sure that the problems which exist in this country at the present time are taken into consideration and corrected with a firm hand. If we will it, it will be so, and if we do not will it, we must recognize that our children and their children will live and die here as serfs.

Norman R. Mancuso, Ph. D.

Natick, Massachusetts

April, 2012

Chapter I

Correcting Our Course

"The real man smiles in trouble; gathers strength from distress, and grows brave by reflection."

Thomas Paine

Guiding the Ship of State

America can be likened to a ship at sea. Without the proper navigational instruments, the captain and crew would have poor knowledge of their location on the globe. As far as is known, the earliest instrument,[6] in its crudest form was the compass, consisting of a magnetized iron needle supported by floats on the surface of a liquid. The direction of the needle, when properly magnetized, roughly indicated North and South. When the needle was parallel to a line, which itself was parallel to the ship's keel, the ship was bearing due North. Occasionally, the needle would have to be re-magnetized by means of a lodestone. This compass was in use by the 13th century.

Some four hundred years later (ca. 1675) the officers of a ship could also use a crude instrument known as a "cross-staff", which was the precursor to the sextant (ca. 1730) by which they could determine the approximate latitude of the vessel. Even prior to Columbus, mariners knew that the determination of Longitude at sea required an accurate knowledge of the time at some standard meridian such as Greenwich, England. However, no other instrument in use at the time would allow the ship's officers to determine the longitude of the vessel at any given place.

"Discovering" Longitude at Sea

Finally, in 1714, the British Admiralty created a commission for "The Discovery of Longitude at Sea". A prize of £20,000 (over $100,000 at that time) was offered for the solution to this problem. The Astronomer Royal and other people contended for this prize, some using a process known as the method of lunar distances. The practical solution however, turned out to be a ticking device in a box, the work of a Yorkshire carpenter named John Harrison. Harrison's solution was based on the contention that if the ship had an accurate timepiece on board, set at the time of the original point of departure, and maintained periodically, the longitude of the vessel could be determined. (It is of interest to note that Harrison was not fully paid until about 1773, almost 60 years after the prize was announced.)

This timepiece would have to be kept wound by an officer on the ship assigned to that duty by the captain, so that it was never in danger of stopping. In addition, the chronometer in use would have to be corrected daily for its gain or loss. To accomplish this, it was necessary to use a chart provided by the maker of the chronograph, who had previously determined the gain or loss of seconds or fractions of a second per hour or day. By using this timepiece, the captain and crew would always know the longitude of the ship relative to that of its home port. Therefore by means of the sextant reading and the timepiece, both read simultaneously, as well as the also-simultaneous compass reading, the captain and officers of a vessel could accurately determine their position at sea. The sextant had provided the latitude of the vessel, the chronograph the simultaneous longitude and the compass, the simultaneous magnetic bearing.

Of course, this book is not about navigation. Nevertheless, an additional point or two in this brief navigational analogy are worth making. A rudderless ship, with or without the proper instrumentation, would be unable to set and maintain a course for a desired destination. On the other hand, a vessel with a rudder but without the proper navigational instrumentation would be capable of maintaining a direction (heading), but would have no way of knowing what course to set. This appears to be the condition of our nation. Our ship of state appears to have a captain and lesser officers as well as a crew, but seems unable to set and maintain a proper course. Whether this is through willfulness or genuine ignorance is an issue of great concern.

If ignorance is the issue, then we are well advised to seek a more intelligent captain and crew. If, on the other hand, the issue is willfulness, then we must determine whether that willfulness is malicious in origin or whether it is simply due to poor or misguided advice. In any event, it seems clear that the United States is being navigated toward the formation of an increasingly socialist state. Moreover, it seems to this observer that the direction being taken is intentional and self-serving. Before we address these issues further, it is prudent to step back and look intently at the nature of the misguided path culminating in a socialist government. It seems impossible to this observer that anyone of average intelligence who has lived through the past few decades would still have any faith in socialism. Rather, it would seem that such individuals would be more interested in the ability to control the populace than in any true belief in the benefits of socialism.

Problems Facing America

The United States, with a birth rate of 2.1 children per couple[7] has no need for nation building, yet the current administration seeks to place socialist programs into the government's provisions for the people. Amnesty for illegal aliens is a case in point. The Liberal Left has repeatedly said that the US will benefit from legalization of this horde of illegal immigrants by providing our country with widespread diversity of population. This is questionable. However, nothing is said about the gradual destruction of the Rule of Law upon which this country was founded. This will be treated in depth in a later chapter. In addition, numerous entitlement programs also exist in the US and with few exceptions do little to protect the people from the creeping perfidy of socialism. With equally few exceptions, these programs were inaugurated by the Democratic Party and the end is not in sight. Numerous other problems exist within the United States government, which if allowed to continue unabated, will destroy the nature of this great country. These include, in no particular order:

- Reckless and uncontrolled spending;
- Rampant welfare programs;
- Massive greed in government and elsewhere;
- Corruption throughout our Government;
- Socialist Programs;

- Immigration and Sharia Law;
- UN Takeover;

Doubtless a high school student could add to this list without any great effort. As we address these and other issues, we will discover ways in which we can turn the ship of state around, turn it around from wasteful spending, turn it around from greed, turn it around from governmental corruption and also to turn it around from our own demands for more government services. And in this process, we may find ways to turn ourselves around from failures on our part to insist that our duly elected representatives keep the ship of this country on its proper course.

.

Chapter 2

Greed and Fraud

"Government, even in its best state, is but a necessity; in its worst state, an intolerable one."

Thomas Paine

The Plague of Greed

Almost from the beginning of humanity, greed has been recognized and much has been said about it. Gordon Gekko, the Wall Street mogul in the movie of that name, coined the phrase "Greed is good!" ostensibly because he was profiting so greatly from it.

Greed is the third of the so-called seven deadly sins and presumably is the mother of all other sin. It is so widespread that one can say that it is a pandemic. The American Heritage Dictionary defines greed as "a rapacious desire for more than one needs or deserves, as of food, wealth, or power; avarice."[8] From the above definition and its pandemic nature, we can believe that all other sins and crimes may be laid at the foot of the god of greed. It is difficult to pick up a newspaper today without reading an article or editorial that charges someone with a crime based on ever-present greed.

Fraud, on the other hand, appears to make its entrance when greed no longer satisfies or when it produces benefits that are less than commensurate for the effort involved. For example, the state of Massachusetts has recently led its third (in a row, no less) speaker of the house before a tribunal of law for crimes that likewise can be laid at the foot of greed. Similarly, Chicago has sentenced four mayors to prison.[9]

Bernard Madoff created and built a Ponzi scheme of incredible proportions by enticing friends and strangers alike to invest heavily in his dubious idea. Two things are surprising about this. First, in hindsight it is difficult for us to understand how Madoff could possibly spend all the money he acquired. Second, most of the investors in this scheme were themselves reasonably wealthy people. So it begins to look like greed piled on top of greed, and one is forced to wonder how many layers existed in this pyramid of greed.

Greed and Fraud in Public Service

In addition to the dangers of being selected as speaker of the house in Massachusetts or mayor in Chicago, if we begin to look closely at the records compiled by various public officials in the United States, I doubt this book could contain enough pages to do an adequate job of reporting the greed and fraud in public service. It's almost necessary to conclude that greed is a substantial job requirement in this area of employment. In keeping with our earlier assumption that greed is the mother of all crime, it is reasonable to speculate that the practice of minor-league greed eventually leads one into the world of major league crime.

For example, it appears that the soon-to-be US Treasury Secretary Timothy Geithner should have spent more time accurately compiling the records for his income tax reports. Instead, his past job as chairman of the New York Fed, involved shoving tens of billions of federal dollars into Citigroup.[10] Using a questionably structured investment plan, Geithner set it up to allow the government to pay over 100 percent of Citigroup's market value for an ownership of 27 percent of the bank. As Kevin D. Williamson pointed out in the December 19, 2011 issue of *National Review*, "If you can't figure out why you'd pay 100+ percent of the bank's value for 27 percent of it then you just don't understand high finance or high politics."[11]

You may have read of this in a newspaper or may have seen it discussed in a financial news report on television, but I think that the degree of greed involved in this type of operation is simply beyond the ability of the average person to get his mind around. This may simply say that the so-called average person is not so greatly affected by greed.

Williamson goes on to say that if one were to compile a record of "recent congressional insider trading, self-dealing, IPO shenanigans and inexplicably good investment luck, it would fill an entire volume and in fact it has." The book Williamson refers to is *Throw Them All Out: How Politicians and Their Friends Get Rich off Insider Stock Tips, Land Deals, and Cronyism That Would Send the Rest of Us to Prison*, by Peter Schweizer of the Hoover Institution.[12]

The double- and dirty-dealing described in this book are activities outside the realm of greed and visibly in the realm of criminal activities inspired by greed. I wholeheartedly recommend that you read both the Williamson article entitled "Repo Men" and the Schweizer book described above. As you read these materials, remember that Congress effectively exempted itself from insider trading rules by failing to pass legislation criminalizing it. This appears to be a case of planning for greed ahead of schedule. Once again, "Opportunity makes the thief."

I have always maintained that there is enough money to do everything necessary and to do it correctly, if only we could eliminate greed. Until crimes against and betrayals of the very people public servants were elected to serve are severely and quickly punished, not by their colleagues but by the electorate, we cannot hope to see a reduction in those crimes and betrayals.

This lack of reduction in crimes of greed and betrayal is not beyond public observation. *The Verdict*, a publication of the Judicial Watch[13] each year releases a list of the "Top Ten Most Wanted" corrupt politicians. I guess that it would come as a shock for most people, especially most Obamaphiles, to learn that President Obama has made the list for the fifth consecutive year. Judicial Watch President Tom Fitton says that this year it was necessary to add a second category, which he called "Dishonorable Mentions."[14]

In another example, the EPA established a program of "renewable fuel standards." This program is proving to be subject to abuse (read, fraud). In 2009, a company in Maryland, Clean Green Fuel (CGF), began to sell credits to legitimate fuel companies that were unable to meet the quota established by the EPA.[15] This program is equal to the "carbon credits" in the aborted Cap and Trade Legislation. Clean Green Fuel sold credits amounting to twenty-one million gallons of biodiesel, which the company claimed were acquired by sending employees to surrounding area restaurants to collect waste vegetable oil to be converted into fuel. An investigation by EPA established that CGF had the facility neither to collect nor to convert anything. Court documents later established that the owner "made" 9.1 million dollars on these transactions. This was used to purchase over two dozen luxury and sports cars as well as almost 82,000 dollars' worth of diamond jewelry for the Mrs.

The EPA is now hounding the twenty-four oil companies that purchased these credits from CGF, since the law stipulates that the purchaser is responsible for determining the legitimacy of the source company. Write to your congresspeople and senators demanding that they fully rescind the renewable mandate.

A further example of fraud followed by gross prevarication in the face of congressional investigation is the so-called "Fast and Furious" (FandF) gunrunning program mandated by the Justice department, or perhaps higher.[16] "Fast and Furious" was run by the Bureau of Alcohol, Tobacco, Firearms and Explosives (BATFE or ATF), which allowed (*instigated* is a more appropriate word) 2,500 semiautomatic firearms to be purchased by "straw buyers" and "walked" into Mexico, where they were turned over to members of the Mexican drug cartels.

This began at least as early as spring of 2010. On December 14, 2010, illegal alien Mexican criminals killed US Border Patrol Agent Brian Terry. Two of the smuggled guns were later found at the scene of the murder. *CBS News* Reporter Sharyl Attkisson spearheaded the investigation of Operation FandF. Both houses of Congress are separately investigating the allegations involved.

Justice Department Chief, Attorney General Eric Holder, asserts that he did not know of the program until a few days before the press broke the story. After being called to testify several times, the AG continues to stonewall the committee. The Department of Justice has produced fewer than 10 percent of the eighty thousand documents subpoenaed by the House Oversight and Government Reform Committee. Over fifteen pages on this story have been exposed in Wayne LaPierre's *"America Disarmed"* describing the internecine departmental attempts to circumvent the law and Congress.[17]

Washington Examiner columnist Diana West filed this report: "The Obama Administration just sealed the court records on the murder of Federal Agent Brian Terry, whose killers, Mexican drug smugglers, used weapons from a failed Federal program, 'Fast and Furious' to smuggle arms into Mexico." [18]

Judicial Watch noted that no one will ever know the reason the public records were sealed in this case, "because the judge's decision to seal it was also sealed."[19]

The following example is more in the category of attempted fraud, since the perpetrators were caught. Each year, the IRS must send Congress a record of the number of tax delinquents in each government agency. Table one, below, lists most of the statistics. The number of federal employees who are delinquent has increased by 13 percent over the last 3.25 years. Rep. Jason Chaffetz has said, "No one who refuses to pay taxes should be allowed to stay in those cushy, overpaid federal positions."[20]

The final example, the practice of lobbying, seems to be a combination of both greed and fraud, with the individual components shared by two different persons. Lobbying is the attempt of an individual or a group to influence legislation, formerly in the public rooms that were then next to the assembly chambers of a legislative group.Today, lobbying may take place anywhere the two interested persons decide to meet. A lobbyist influences legislators to introduce or support legislation that is favorable to the group who has paid that person.

Table I
Government Employees Delinquent
in Payment of Income Taxes

Gov't. Agency	# or % Delinquent	Total of Unpaid Taxes
Office of Gov. Ethics	6.5%	
Gov. Accountability Office	65	
Fed. Reserve Bd. of Governors	91	$1,265,152
Office of Personnel Management		$1,917,149
U.S. Tax Court		$62,508
Sec. & Exchange Commission		$1,146,843
Postal Service	25,640	$269,641,265
Soc.Sec. Administration		$20,144,559
House of Representatives	467	$8,535,974
Senate	217	$2,134,501
Exec. Office of the President	36	$833,970

Usually this is under the guise of supporting a legislator either with money, usually to affect his or her reelection, or with favors of various worth. The recurring need for capital to finance reelection is often the driving factor that entices a legislator to accept such gifts. It may or may not be dishonest or greedy to accept such monies, but the giving of those monies by lobbyists usually is dishonest and may be a fraudulent act. Nevertheless, such lobbying is a fact of political life in almost every political entity on earth.

Corporate Greed and Fraud

Gordon Gekko is not alone. All of us have heard about the wide divergence between what corporate executives and low-level employees are paid. Some of this is justified by the value placed on a person who is able to influence the bottom line of a company strongly, and this is perhaps warranted. Nonetheless, most of this deep-pocket remuneration is not justifiable.

Other issues, such as the recent Solyndra scandal,[21] raise a stench in the nostrils of all honest citizens. It borders on the unimaginable that there is no more *quid pro quo* than is insinuated. Are we expected to believe that each act of such dishonesty is so hidden as to escape the wide-open eyes of even teenagers? What message does this send to those same teenagers, who witness our country's so-called leaders profit personally from such disgustingly obvious political shenanigans? Is it even possible to look the other way? No matter how much we may try to direct the morals of our youngsters, daily contact with any Internet sites or TV news programs will easily redirect them, which are good examples by which to learn greed and even pursue further education in the realm of fraud.

The Voting Booth Is Always Available

Today there are many ways to contact your legislators, and most cost little or nothing. Don't think that they do not heed what their constituents tell them. Their staff keeps accurate records of all the issues constituents bring to their attention. Pros and cons are recorded on every issue of importance to you and others in your precinct, city, and state. Be prepared by having a draft letter or e-mail to your legislator(s) on your computer. Leave a blank area in which to address the issue that you believe warrants their attention.

Do not hesitate to address your concerns to someone who may not be your representative but who serves on the committee responsible for the issue you are writing about. Formerly, legislators more carefully considered postcards and USPS mail, but now e-mail is faster, cheaper, and just as well received. So if you have access to a computer, get those drafts ready.

The first draft is the hardest, and all others are almost copies. Save them as DraftSenator1, DraftSenator2, etc., for e-mail or word-processing programs. Then choose them as needed, fill in the blank areas, and send them off to the person they are addressed to.

If you do not have a computer, most public libraries do. On the other hand, perhaps a friend will allow you to use his computer. Just take your written drafts and a disk on which to save your drafts and the final letters. Or simply handwrite your letters and accept the inconvenience as the price of good government.

Using this approach, you are able to reach your representatives as often as you require. Insist on a response from the addressee or his or her office staff and if necessary, *remind him or her politely that you vote regularly.*

With regard to the current issue of greed, don't be afraid to address your letter or e-mail directly to the person who displayed this greed. Just remember to be civil and to the point; you are hoping to change the person in question, not alienate him or her. Think about starting your own correspondence group by enlisting a few friends who feel the same way. Don't try to start an e-mailing horde; recruit just a few friends who are willing to support your cause, which should be theirs as well.

You will not be ignored; I promise you. If you want to increase your power a hundredfold, write to the local newspaper as well as the newspaper serving the hometown of the person you are trying to reach. Once again, be reasonable and civil, because you don't want heat, you merely want to cast light on the matter. You can say that you expect better from these civil servants, as do the thousands who do not write letters to the editor.

Once you start to use this technique, you will find that it does not require inordinate amounts of time. You probably learn the news through the media, so you will be armed with reports of all sorts of transgressions that will be arrows for your e-mail or postal bow.

To make this even easier for you, in the appendix I have included a template of such a letter to your representatives.

Chapter 3

Reckless and Profligate Spending

"Moderation in temper is always a virtue; but moderation in principle is always a vice."

Thomas Paine

Background

Governments, like people, have legitimate requirements that make it necessary for them to spend money. They also require a budget in order to bring expenses in line with income. However, unlike you and me, they are not bothered by the necessity of a balanced budget, as you have no doubt heard many times. Governments use a metric for the current productive value of their country, called the Gross Domestic Product (GDP) which, in principle, is similar to what total income is to the average person. It is defined as the total amount in dollars (or other currency) of all goods produced and all services rendered within the country. The GDP of the United States in 2011 was about 15.3 trillion dollars.[22]

When spending exceeds a certain percentage of the GDP, governments must increase their income sufficiently to pay for their spending plans. (See the discussion of the Cut, Cap, and Balance Act, later in this chapter.) They can do this in a number of ways, such as additional taxation, borrowing money, raising tariffs, or deficit spending. We are all familiar with the first two approaches to augmenting the government's total income. Raising tariffs is likely to cause similar responses from those countries affected by the first raise and so, in many cases, it turns out to be revenue neutral.

Anyone who has bounced a check also knows what deficit spending is, but for those few lucky people who have not, here's a definition: deficit spending is the process of spending money without having the money to spend. For the average person, deficit spending ultimately results in bankruptcy, because eventually that person exceeds his or her credit limits.

Some economists believe that it is possible for a country to go on deficit spending indefinitely; in other words, apparently, there is no possibility for a country to descend into bankruptcy. Eventually it will become necessary to cover your spending with some sort of cash or other form of payment. Governments, like people, require a source of credit by which they can finance their spending activities. Also, like people, governments can borrow from themselves as long as they have the surplus to cover it. The question is, Is it a genuine surplus? The real answer to all this is that, eventually, you will have to pay the piper.

US Historical Spending

Having said all of the previous, it is still necessary to investigate where we are spending our reserves and where we are borrowing to replace our losses. Obviously, we are already borrowing heavily from our future income, and there is a limit on how much we can continue to borrow from our citizens. Raising taxes is not a viable option, since very soon it would raise an enormous outcry against the federal government as well as both houses of Congress. So the government's source of credit must include an external money supply. Before we determine where that money supply is, let's first look at how much we are spending.[23]

Again, the rate of spending began to increase greatly beginning in 1933, a few years after the Great Depression and coincidentally, perhaps, at the beginning of the so-called New Deal; it remains for us to determine why we began to spend so heavily at that point. History has shown that during every war, spending as a percent of the GDP increases sharply. And, after every war, it takes time to recover—and it never returns to the pre-bellum rate of spending. However, if we ignore World War I and the Great Depression, the rate of spending did not significantly increase. Once again, ignoring the effect of World War II and the Korean conflict, we can see that we are already beginning the era of profligate spending.

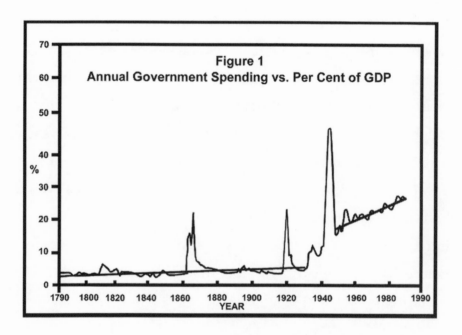

Figure 1
Annual Government Spending vs. Per Cent of GDP

Spending and Borrowing

Figure one, above,[24] illustrates the spending of the US government for two hundred years, from 1790 to 1990 as a percentage of GDP. Prior to the Great Depression, government spending averaged less than about 3.5 percent of the GDP (see the long, slowly rising flat line). This encompassed the period from 1790 to 1933 and excludes those years or periods during which the United States was at war. Beginning in 1933, it leapt to about 10 percent of the GDP, and except for a very brief return to about 6.5 percent of the GDP, it never again returned to this level. Excluding WWII, it then began to rise at a rate of 0.5 percent of the GDP annually. In 1990, it culminated at about 23 to 24 percent of the GDP. Excluding WWII and the Korean "police action," the United States began to spend at a prodigious rate that is unexplained by any of the economic theories available at this time, with the possible exception of the so-called "rent-seeking" phenomenon.[25] "Rent seeking" is the term coined by economists for the process wherein special-interest groups lobby the government to transfer wealth to them. (Please see the chapter on greed.)

I have always maintained, more as a gut feeling than as a special insight, that there is always enough money to do everything and always enough to do everything *right*, if greed, fraud, earmarks, special-interest amendments, lobbying, and other similar factors could be eliminated. Although this is not the entire picture, for now, accept it.

Total government spending increased from about 10 billion dollars in 1930 to 5.92 trillion dollars in 2010. To those not versatile in math, this is a 592 times the 1930 rate. The federal deficit in 1930 was essentially zero and grew to a mind-boggling 1.3 trillion dollars in 2010. To provide even greater perspective, in 2000 there was a surplus of 200 billion dollars. Somehow, in ten years, we seem to have borrowed our way through about 1.5 trillion dollars.

This gross public debt figure should cause everyone to lose his or her self-control. We are now indebted to the tune of *16 trillion dollars.* If things continue at the current rate, we will very soon find out whether or not countries can go bankrupt. Greece has come close, and God forbid, we might follow or exceed them.

If you follow media reports, you must be aware that the United States is heavily indebted to China. The Chinese government has incredible amounts of cash available and is only too willing to extend credit to the United States. The current US debt owned by the People's Republic is approximately one-quarter of the total US debt. It's difficult to say with any degree of certainty what prompts the largesse of the Chinese government to buy up such large amounts of American "paper." I cannot recall the author who first coined the following phrase, but I do recall the message: "There are only two kinds of people in the world, those who think that they understand the Oriental psyche and those who know that they do not."

The US government is not opposed to raising taxes. This is particularly true of the Democratic administrations and notoriously true of the Obama administration. In 2010, Obama himself created the Bowles-Simpson commission.[26] Rather than accept the recommendation of the Bowles-Simpson commission, he once more attempted to create division within the various tax groups by stressing the fact that the current tax laws favor millionaires over middle-income persons and families.

In his State of the Union address, Obama proposed the so-called Buffett Rule, which establishes a taxation floor of 30 percent but does nothing to establish a taxation ceiling. The Bowles-Simpson proposal went in exactly the opposite direction by saying, "The top rate must not exceed 29 percent." And even more to their credit, the writers of Bowles-Simpson proposed that federal spending be capped at 21 percent of the GDP. The Democrats rejected this. Clearly, Obama didn't have any interest in a plan that boxes him in on taxes. Rather, he revealed his long-term vision of a high-tax, high-spend America.[27]

President Obama failed to assert that the top-tier income groups continually invest and produce from the private economy rather than requiring funding from the federal government.

Investing by the higher-income groups creates an economy built to last, and the Buffett Rule will create an economy built to fail.

Table II More Spending Kills Jobs		
YEARS	CHANGE IN GOV. SPENDING AS % GDP	% CHANGE IN LABOR FORCE AT WORK
1929-1939	+283	-15.0
1946-1951	-15	+3.3
1954-1973	-13	+2.3
1973-1982	+28	0.0
1982-2000	-26	+6.5
2000-2007	+7	-1.4
2007-2011	+18	-4.6

Table II, above, illustrates that as government spending as percent of GDP increases, the change in the labor force at work decreases.[28] [Table II is reconstructed from the *Washington Times* Weekend Edition from data provided by CBO, BLS, US Census, and Richard Rahn.] This is an inverse relationship, which is exactly the opposite of what neo-Keynesian economists have repeatedly predicted. Taxing the wealthy is the wrong, wrong, wrong way to go. Increasing the labor force at work puts money back into the hands of the poor and the middle class by creating jobs. The wealthy may benefit through lower taxes, but the other classes benefit by having a paycheck. Why do the Democrats refuse to learn this simple lesson?

Military (Defense) Spending

During the quests of special-interest groups for their "slice of the government pie," one always seems to hear that defense spending consumes wildly exaggerated amounts of money. To be sure, the wars in Iraq and Afghanistan consumed a significant amount of this money. However, military spending (MS)[29] in peacetime usually does not amount to more than 6 percent of the GDP. For example, in 2001, MS was at a low of 3.6 percent (all percentages in this section refer to amounts relative to the GDP). From 2005 to 2007, it reached about 4.75 percent, and in 2011, it reached a high of almost 6 percent. It is estimated that in 2015, MS will recede once more to about 4.8 percent.

It is interesting that once a war is over, MS never recedes to the value that existed prior to the commencement of hostilities. Perhaps this is because war points out shortcomings of certain war materiel, and the additional MS is required to correct these and other known or incipient problems. In any event, it seems clear that MS is not a major contributor to government spending.[30] The estimated total of MS for 2012 is approximately 5+ percent.

The Cost of Government

The actual cost of government—that is, the amount of money spent by the government in the pursuit of its activities—is exceedingly difficult to determine. That is because, for the most part, it lies buried in the individual line items that make up the total budget for the year.

An interesting paper by the Heritage Foundation[31] attempts to determine what these costs are. It is well worth reading in its entirety to determine what the actual cost of the federal government is. The following excerpt is itself extremely enlightening:

> Many people may think that regulatory costs are a business problem. Indeed, they are, but the costs of regulation are inevitably passed on to consumers in the form of higher prices and limited product choices. Basic items such as toilets, shower heads, light bulbs, mattresses, washing machines, dryers, cars, ovens, refrigerators, televisions sets, and bicycles, all cost significantly more because of government decrees on energy use, product labeling, and performance standards that go well beyond safety, as well as hundreds of millions of hours of testing and paperwork to document compliance.
>
> There is no official accounting of total regulatory costs, and estimates vary. Unlike the budgetary accounting of direct

tax revenues, Washington does not track the total burdens imposed by its expansive rule-making. An oft-quoted estimate of 1.75 trillion dollars annually, represents nearly twice the amount of individual income taxes collected last year [32]

The report goes on to estimate the costs of regulation for the first half of the year 2011. Also provided is an estimate of additional regulatory costs during the remainder of Obama's first term. Figures provided by the Federal Office of Management and Budget illustrate that well over 100 billion dollars of these costs would directly affect businesses. Moreover, costs to implement these regulations are rarely, if ever, calculated, and do not include the internal work to ensure regulatory compliance, estimated to be several tens of thousands of hours.

Obama is the first US president to burden businesses and individuals with a higher number and greater cost of regulations in the same period as that of the preceding administration.[33] The Heritage Foundation paper goes on to recommend three sweeping reforms:

- Require Congressional approval of new major rules promulgated by agencies. (A major rule is one which will have an economic impact of at least 100 million dollars.)

- Create a Congressional Office of Regulatory Analysis. (This would be an independent group modeled on the Congressional Budget Office and responsible only to congress.)
- Establish a Sunset Date for federal regulations

President Obama and like-minded Democrats or Republicans—those with a tax-and-spend philosophy—must not be allowed to regain public office. Indeed, that philosophy has snowballed into a borrow-and-spend mentality, since spending currently exceeds twice the income revenue from taxpayers. Give heed to the words of Thomas Sowell:

> If you have been voting for politicians who promise to give you goodies at someone else's expense, then you have no right to complain when they take your money and give it to someone else, including themselves.[34]

To this I might add, politicians of any party who promise to reduce the size of government and fail to do so should be pressured in every conceivable manner, even recall, if unresponsive to other attempts.

The Growth of Government

The above facts are difficult enough to digest. What follows will send you running for Zantac, Tums, or whatever you consume to combat an attack of *aceto*. *Investor's Business Daily* has reported that 22.5 million Americans now work for government, more than manufacturing, farming, and fishing combined.[35] The three occupations listed above are among those that actively produce wealth; only mining is not included. Moreover, the average compensation (wages and benefits) of federal civilian employees is 119,982 dollars. The annual total of federal payroll and benefits would therefore be very close to 2.7 trillion dollars. I say! Can we possibly be getting our money's worth?

These figures are hard to believe, so let us pursue this issue further. In an article entitled "Leviathan" in National Review Online, the author attempts to determine this for himself. His research shows that in 2009, the federal government (FG) employed 2.8 million out of a total work force of 236 million, over 1 percent.[36] Add uniformed military personnel, and the figure increases to 4.4 million, and there are sixty-six thousand people working in the legislative branch and federal courts, bringing the total to around 2 percent. Think we're done now? Hardly.

Professor Paul Light of New York University has estimated the size of the "shadow" government, which includes those who work for contractors and grantees, those paid through government-funded research grants. The Office of Personnel Management (OPM) has failed to keep track of these figures, perhaps because this would allow the FG to estimate actual labor costs. So much for the "transparency" we were supposed to see under this president.

Nevertheless, Light used the FG's procurement database to ascertain useful estimates. His figures show that the true size of the FG was about 11 million. Just as the TV commercial says, "And that's not all!" Further research into the size of the "shadow" government shows that the total true size of the FG is a whopping twenty million, which compares quite well with the previous figure quoted.[37] The possibly deliberate obfuscation of all the numbers makes it exceedingly difficult to determine the actual cost of government—which the FG does little to dispel.

In any event, at the current rates, the size of the government at all levels, will take up more than half of all economic activity by 2050. In other words, the cost of government will be 50 percent of GDP. If we are borrowing forty-three cents out of every dollar at the present time, how many Chinese Yuan will be coming across the ocean for every dollar we spend? Not to worry, because we will probably all be busy studying Mandarin or some other Chinese dialect by that time.

A Comparison of Federal Vs. Private Sector

Figure two, below, compares federal workers' average compensation relative to private sector similar positions.[38] Compensation includes both wages and benefits, and only includes a comparison for civilian workers in both FG and the private sector. So multiplying the number of FG civilian workers (2.8 million) by the value given for them in figure 2, (119,982 dollars) gives a line item for "Salaries and benefits for FG civilian worker" of over 335 billion dollars.

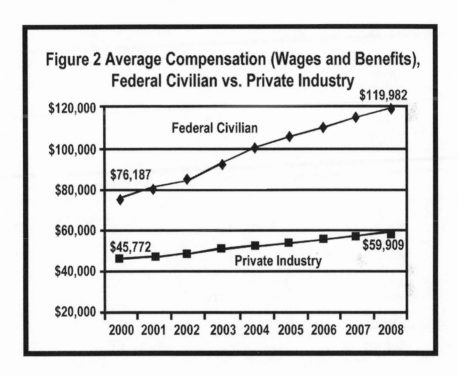

Figure 2 Average Compensation (Wages and Benefits), Federal Civilian vs. Private Industry

As you can see, it is almost impossible to acquire the total salary and benefit figure (as previously obtained for regular government employees) which now includes grantees, "shadow" employees, military, postal, and other ancillary FG employees. If similar state and local employees are included, Light's total of 20 million FG employees has grown by an additional 19.5 million state and local government employees and gives us half of the equation[39].

But unfortunately we are missing the corrected value for the other half—namely, the average salary for all of these ancillary government workers. It is a safe bet that a great number of accountants would be required and the values obtained would be at least a number of years too late.

There is enough additional data to swell this chapter to gargantuan proportions, but little is gained from this except to tax the reader's patience and perseverance. However, one additional section must be included—namely, the solution to this chronic problem.

The Cut, Cap, and Balance Act

The somewhat unusual title of this section is perhaps the future solution to reining in the debt that follows this level of government spending. I will attempt to describe the benefits and impositions of this bill, HR 2560, the Cut, Cap and Balance Act.[40]

Title I of this bill cuts discretionary spending by prohibiting the House or Senate from considering any bill that would increase discretionary spending beyond limits set forth in the bill.[41]

Title II of this bill places a cap on total spending after fiscal year (FY) 2012, as a percentage of GDP, as estimated by the OMB. The caps range from 21.7 percent in FY 2013 to 18.0 percent in FY 2022.

Title III of this bill is a Balanced Budget Amendment (BBA) to the Constitution. HR 2560 would prohibit the secretary of the treasury from increasing the debt limit until the archivist of the United States has transmitted to the chambers of the Congress, a qualifying BBA to the Constitution that has been approved in both chambers and is ready for ratification by the states. There are, at present, three versions of the BBA that would qualify:

- SJ Res. 10 Sponsored by Sen. Hatch (R-UT) with 47 Senate co-sponsors
- HJ Res. 56 Sponsored by Rep. Walsh (R-IL) with 59 House co-sponsors
- HJ Res. 1 Sponsored by Rep. Goodlatte (R-VA) with 133 House co-sponsors

According to the *Wall Street Journal,*

Congress has never failed to increase the debt limit. This makes having a debt limit functionally useless... Republicans in the Bush years and Democrats in the Obama years have proven that we cannot trust them when it comes to spending...*The current Congress has a chance to do right by the next generation. Now more than ever, we need politicians who will risk their political careers with courage, to do what must be done.* (Emphasis added.)[42]

Chapter 4

Fixing Social Security

"A long habit of not thinking a thing wrong, gives it the superficial appearance of being right."

Thomas Paine

Social Security Background

The Social Security fund was designed to provide a measure of retirement income for the average person who paid into this tax fund from his or her current income. It was signed into law by Franklin Roosevelt in 1935 as a part of the so-called New Deal. This program was to be known as the Federal Income Contribution Act (FICA). The plan was that wage earners would contribute a percentage of their income to FICA, and this tax would be matched by a similar contribution from each person's employer. This would be invested and would hopefully grow into a sizable sum, which would ultimately provide income for the individual. The plan started as a contribution of 1.0 percent of the first three thousand dollars of the employee's wages matched by a like amount from the employer. For 2010, the employee contributed 7.65 percent for FICA on the first 106,800 dollars and 1.45 percent (with no limit) for Medicare. The employer contributes a like amount. The 2011 reduced amount was continued until February 2012 and is now to be continued to the end of 2012.

Originally, the plan was that the government would invest the monies collected from both the employer and the employee. It is difficult to determine accurately just what the original plan meant when it referred to "investing." Today the term generally means depositing money into one of the many financial markets available to the investor. However, at that time, the plan was pay-as-you-go: the benefits due were paid out of the incoming Social Security funds, and the funds remaining were invested in a special Social Security trust fund. The managing trustee of the fund was the secretary of the treasury, who was allowed to invest funds in both marketable and nonmarketable securities. The money in the trust fund was secured by special government bonds that were not available to the public.

The Rape of Social Security

These special Social Security bonds were backed by "the full faith and credit of the United States Government." However, in setting up the Social Security trust fund in this manner, the money in the trust fund was essentially loaned back to the federal government to pay for other expenses. This means the government has created the tax on anyone who holds down a job, ostensibly to provide him or her with an income in his or her retired years.

Since it is pay-as-you-go, the money received is payed to individuals who have retired, according to their actuarially determined benefits. The remaining money is invested in the aforementioned government bonds. Many shortfalls have happened in the intervening years and each time a shortfall cropped up, the legislature passed a bill that tried to set the Social Security system aright. From 1982 on, tax receipts, interest payments, and other income have exceeded benefit payments as well as other expenditures. In 2004, this excess amounted to more than 150 billion dollars. The bad news is that it was then projected that, by 2036, the trust fund and all of its excess would be exhausted.

Unless something is quickly done about this, excessive increases in taxation and the almost equivalently excessive decreases in benefits will greet newly retired persons. In fact, a recent *Washington Times* article stated that by 2022, Social

Security reserves will run dry, according to President Obama's federal budget released on February 13, 2012.[43] How could such a thing have happened? Only by tricks and government legerdemain can such things occur. The law was changed in 1983 and again in 1990 in a manner that was supposed to provide additional income, which resulted in a large short-term surplus of funds. This surplus was invested in a special Treasury bond unavailable to the public, but not beyond the reach of Congress.

In 2009, the Office of the Chief Actuary of the Social Security Administration calculated that there was an "unfunded obligation" of 15.1 trillion dollars for the Social Security program. The "unfunded obligation" (UO) equals the present value of the current cost of SS (CC) minus the sum of present value of the trust fund assets (TFA) plus the future scheduled tax income (FTI) of the program. It may be clearer to describe this mathematically:

$$UO = CC - (TFA + FTI)$$

In determining what happened to the trust fund, it must be remembered that buying treasury bonds is akin to placing that income into the general coffers of the government. Congress and the administration are free to use that to finance deficit spending, provided that any monies used are replaced with a government IOU.

Tiffany N. Anthony, "The All-American Black Girl", as she describes herself, lists a number of Social Security Fund abuses, replete with references. These include[44]:

- 100,000 dollars for a Punxsutawney, Pennsylvania, museum (home of Phil, the groundhog.)
- 20 million dollars for the Presidio Trust to transform the old army base into a national park.
- 25,000 dollars for the Las Vegas schools to study Mariachi music.
- 400,000 dollars for the Charity Cultural Services Center for a "Skills for Life Program for Asian Immigrants"
- 591,000 dollars for The International Women's Museum espoused by Nancy Pelosi and Barbara Boxer

Government Social Security Reforms

Fortunately, the Social Security Advisory Board has appointed a Technical Advisory Panel (TAP), whose responsibility is to include a review of the methods and assumptions used in the annual projections and to propose alternative legislation by means of which the Social Security system can be rescued. Several proposals from TAP, as well as from other organizations and private individuals, have been made.[45-50] Most of these involve the same basic principles—for example, either privatization of all or portions of retirement funds as well as other approaches similar to an improved Social Security system, in addition to combinations of these two types of programs.

Experiments involving privatization, which had been started many years earlier, have been studied and found to be very promising. However, the recession that started in 2008 has produced a significant amount of fear about what would happen to a private pension plan in these market conditions.

(George W. Bush has had his hand slapped, in a figurative sense, when President Obama repeatedly blamed him for the crisis Obama claims to have inherited. The truth is that the reason for the 2008 meltdown of the subprime mortgage debacle began in the Clinton administration,[51] and this is where the blame should be placed.)

It is beyond the scope of this work to examine and report on the details of each of these plans. The concerned reader should consult the references given for details. Anyone who reads this section and feels concern about the future of Social Security should turn to the section entitled "The Voting Booth Is Always Available" in chapter two and take appropriate action.

Chapter 5

Welfare and Reform

"We still find the greedy hand of government thrusting itself into every corner and crevice of industry and grasping at the spoil of the multitude. Invention is continually exercised to furnish new pretenses for revenue and taxation."

Thomas Paine

In the Beginning

What we know today as welfare actually started after the crash of 1929 and the start of the subsequent Depression. It was known then as *relief*. It was part of the so-called New Deal proposed by Franklin Roosevelt to prevent the Depression from getting out of hand. However, even as late as post-World War II, to say that someone "was on relief" or had "taken relief funds" was a pejorative that was not accepted either mildly or willingly.

Welfare was started primarily to aid the destitute—that is, those without income or other resources, probably with the hope of preventing those citizens from dropping into a criminal occupation to stave off starvation and other results of poverty. When I was eight years old, I witnessed one man telling another that he (the other) had taken relief and this quickly resulted in a physical altercation. So, in those days, it was not readily accepted.

It is also necessary to remember that welfare or relief was nothing more than what many of us, Christians or otherwise, called Christian charity. This was nothing more than coming to the aid of another person or persons who were in genuine need of help from others. However, relief or welfare was delivered by the government.

The Failed Beginning of Reform

In 1933 Franklin Delano Roosevelt, a Democrat, signed into law the New Deal, which contained the provisions for relief. Scarcely two years after passing the law, FDR recognized that relief had the capacity to end up as a blight on the social landscape. In 1935, he said:

> Continued dependence upon relief induces a spiritual and moral disintegration fundamentally destructive to the national fibre (*sic*). To dole out relief in this way is to administer a narcotic, a subtle destroyer of the human spirit.

However, it was continued unabated. It should be obvious that welfare as we know it began at this time. At about 1950, total welfare spending has increased from about ten to fifteen billion dollars to about 705 billion dollars in 2008. (Both figures are in 2008 inflation-adjusted dollars.)

In 1964 President Lyndon Johnson, also a Democrat, launched the so-called War on Poverty. This was a means-tested program, which indicates that the recipient of the benefits had complied with certain requirements in order to receive benefits. Unfortunately, the "war" proceeded disastrously, with the government as the main casualty, resulting in spending sufficient money to remove every family from poverty. But that result never occurred; the poverty rate continued to increase. From about 1981 to 1990, the poverty rate leveled off substantially under President Ronald Reagan.

However, from 1990 to 1995, the rate grew exponentially under the so-called Aid to Families with Dependent Children (AFDC). Finally, in 1996, the AFDC was replaced with another program called Temporary Assistance to Needy Families (TANF), which held the poverty rate steady until about 1999.

The Current State of Affairs

Nevertheless, the rate of growth of welfare spending is not sustainable and will result in the United States entering bankruptcy if it is allowed to continue. According to the Heritage Foundation, since the 1960s, the United States has spent about sixteen trillion dollars on welfare, and over the next ten years, it is projected to cost an additional 10.3 trillion dollars.[52] It is the fastest-growing part of our economy and results in spending much more on welfare than on national defense.

The question that comes to mind is, How did this happen? As with any complicated issue, there are several answers. The first and probably the most significant answer results from asking, Who are these poor? For example, the Census Bureau reported in 2010 that forty-three million Americans were categorized as poor. This is more than one in every eight Americans—an astonishingly large number compared to what one might suspect. How might we rationalize the difference between what we would suspect and what the Census Bureau has revealed? The first thing that comes to mind and probably the most important answer, based on real numbers, is that definitions of *poor* are quite different. A thorough report by Robert Rector and Kirk Johnson states the following:

> The typical American defined as poor by the government has a car, air conditioning, a refrigerator, a stove, a clothes washer and dryer, and a microwave. He has two color televisions, cable or satellite TV reception, a VCR or DVD player, and a stereo. He is able to obtain medical care. His home is in good repair and is not crowded. By his own report, his family is not hungry and he had sufficient funds in the past year to meet his family's essential needs. While this individual's life is not opulent, it is equally far from the popular images of dire poverty conveyed by the press, liberal activists, and politicians...The best news is that remaining poverty can readily be reduced, particularly among children. There are two main reasons that American children are poor: Their parents don't work much and fathers are absent from the home.[53]

It should be possible to go after these delinquent fathers in the same manner in which states pursue "deadbeat dads." If a woman refuses to identify the father of a child, birth records usually show both sides of a child's parentage. Chasing down these men—or women, as the case may be—and prosecuting them for child support seems to be a worthwhile endeavor. Further, failure of these men or women to acknowledge their responsibility or failure to report periodically to social case workers, should be grounds to pursue other legal options.

In any case, welfare reform is a requirement and should be pursued vigorously. Yes, it is a very difficult row to hoe, but in its present form, it will be the doom of America.

Other Entitlement Programs

Another possible reason for this large number of "poor" people may be that those who determine whether a person or family is poor are unable to deal with the applicant's assertion of poverty in a negative or realistic way. By this I mean that, when confronted with someone who claims to be poor, the person doing the interviewing is unable to say, "No, you are not poor according to the standards I must use." It is far easier to say, "Yes, of course, I understand," and simply to add that person or family to the rolls of the poor. This will permit the interviewer to turn a potentially uncomfortable situation into one in which both parties are relieved.

Of course, it is not easy to judge a situation like this without knowing firsthand the characteristics of the interviewers. Also, it is entirely possible that the interviewers' supervisors instruct them on certain criteria and tell them not deviate from them. In this case, even those interviewers who are capable of dealing critically with the claimants are restrained from doing so.

In any discussion of welfare, questions come up relating to the extent of welfare fraud. Very few figures are available on this issue. In a somewhat cursory search of the Internet, I repeatedly came up with a figure of 1 to 2 percent. These are supposedly "proven" cases of fraud, and in one report, it was the number of cases from which a monetary judgment was achieved.

However, this is a drop in the bucket compared to the total cost of the problem. Although none of us would turn down 1 percent of a trillion dollars (that is, ten billion dollars), that's a significant amount relative to the total. I believe that the figure of 1 percent is low, but it seems unrealistic, in the absence of evidence, to offer a figure greater than 5 percent. It is difficult to get a fix on the cost of welfare fraud because the enforcement of this problem is left to individual states. Consequently, it is difficult to find an entry under welfare fraud on the Internet that is not associated with a state agency.

On the other hand, since it is a state problem, one must find out what 1 percent of the total cost is for all fifty states. An estimate can be obtained based on 2008 figures, when the total welfare cost for all fifty states was 714 billion dollars. One percent of that amount would be 7.14 billion and 10 percent is 71.4 billion. Neither amount should be dismissed.

This is akin to the problem of determining the total salary of all government employees. The data is there but scattered so widely that it is not possible to determine an accurate number. It would seem that, to obtain and correlate this information, an annual reporting system to the federal government would not be beyond the capabilities of the individual states nor of the federal government. A recent report on *ABC World News* estimated that Medicare and Medicaid fraud amounted to 10 percent. However, no mention was made of the source of this figure.[54] In 2008, total medical welfare was 372 billion dollars. Presuming that all of this was the sum of both Medicare and Medicaid, and the 10 percent was attributable to both programs, the total cost of fraud would have been 37.2 billion dollars.

Finally, in great measure, the Democrats have sponsored the legislation that has placed us in the welfare situation we are in today. (It's said that Obama has added 40 percent to the Food Stamp Program, while others say that Bush has added a larger number. What is not said is that Bush's increase of 14.7 million persons took place over eight years (ca. 1.84 million per year); while Obama has added 14.2 million over about three years (ca. 4.9 million per year.) The full story is in the following.) Moreover, the administration may have done this, at least in part, to permit the Democratic Party to engage and control a large voting block that will ultimately be used either to elect more Democrats in future elections or to figure into polls or other pro-administration actions.[55]

The most important point to be remembered is that you, and especially your children, will be mortgaged to the hilt to pay for the rampant increase in spending required to finance government spending in general or the welfare debacle in particular. Unless potent legislation is passed that substantially reduces the number of people on the government dole, within the next decade, America, as we know it, will be gone. If anything is left, all that will remain will be a nation of paupers. I wonder who will come to our aid.

Chapter 6

US Sovereignty

"The duty of a patriot is to protect his country from its government."

Thomas Paine

United Nations Background

Protection of US sovereignty is one of the most serious problems, if not absolutely the most serious problem, facing the United States of America today. The United Nations (UN), the child of an innocent United States, has turned on its founder and chief financier in a manner befitting a true Benedict Arnold. Founded in 1945, after World War II, by FDR to replace the ineffective League of Nations, the United Nations includes 193 member states. The current secretary-general is Ban Ki-moon of South Korea. The United States provides 22 percent of the total UN budget. For FY 2012, this amounts to over 568 million dollars out of a total 2.4 billion dollars.

During the past several years, the United Nations has been clearly aiming at a one-world government (described in the next sections) to be the supranational head of all independent states, including the United States. Barack Obama has just informed the Senate Foreign Relations Committee that there are seventeen UN treaties he wants ratified. (These are also detailed in the following sections of this chapter.) All of these are designed to erode US sovereignty. And that is for one reason only: that the UN people in charge of the plan for a world order realize that the United States is the single greatest roadblock to their plans. Therefore, it is of major importance to destroy the constitutional government of the United States before it fully derails UN plans.

United Nations World Taxation

In addition to the member-nation taxation used to finance the United Nations operations, the socialists at the United Nations have issued a report demanding that UN global taxes be imposed. The National Committee against the UN Takeover[56] has stated that the author of the UN Global Tax Report, now funded by billionaire George Soros, a radical leftist, is working with the

Occupy Wall Street socialists. The purpose of this liaison is to continue to demand a UN global tax. They are joined by leftist members of Congress who have submitted similar legislation.

When he was a senator, Barack Obama also sponsored similar legislation. *Reuters* reported, "The president made clear that he shares the objectives" of the European leaders demanding global taxes. In addition, the president recently met with international socialist unions, who are in the forefront of the campaign for UN global taxes.

Pat Coniff, who is the executive director of the US Freedom Fund,[57] stated that UN Secretary-General Ban Ki-moon is doing everything in his power to force his one-world UN government on America by destroying our economy. The United Nations intend to do this by imposing a tax on all US financial transactions occurring anywhere in the world. This tax would apply every time you write a check, withdraw money from your bank accounts, and accrue interest on your savings accounts. There is currently a house bill, HR 1146, authored by Rep. Ron Paul that seeks to prevent this.[58] Unfortunately it is currently stalled in committee.

Obama-Clinton UN Treaty Agenda

President Obama and Secretary of State Hillary Clinton have compiled a list of the UN treaties that they want ratified by the Senate and the states of the United States. The list below is not comprehensive. Neither are the ramifications. However, there are enough frightening items on this list to bleach the complexion of every American who hears of them.[59]

- Foreign law will replace the US Constitution.
- The United Nations will impose global taxes on Americans.
- The United Nations will take control of all off-shore US oil resources.
- The United Nations will dictate where US naval vessels may go.
- The United Nations will overturn the US Second Amendment.
- The United Nations wants all US reservations against any UN treaty nullified. [When a sovereign nation accepts a United Nations treaty, it may do so with reservations, e.g., to protect it's citizens from any United Nations law that contravenes that nation's laws. Having done so, the sovereign nation may later choose to remove the reservation it had previously imposed.]
- The United Nations will impose a non-verifiable, comprehensive nuclear test ban.
- The United Nations will impose an international criminal court to try and punish US military personnel who may be falsely accused of "war crimes."

- Plus nine other UN treaties that will ultimately end the United States as we know it.

We cannot let this happen. You will recall that Barack Obama, both before and after he was elected president, openly stated that he was in favor of a redistribution of wealth. Since World War I, the United States has redistributed American wealth to many, many countries in humanitarian aid of one sort or another. (See number four below.) Indeed, even the United Nations itself is a redistribution of American wealth.

Also recall that, as reported by Freedom Alliance,[60] Barack Obama stated to a European audience, "I am a citizen of the world." It is clear that these treaties meet his intent. However, you can be equally sure that his wealth and the wealth of his friends are not included in this plan. Many of his sycophant friends will be surprised to find that their wealth may not escape this trap.

Leave the United Nations

The following seven "indisputable" reasons why the United States should remove itself from the United Nations are provided by Jeffrey Gayner, chairman of Americans for Sovereignty.

1. *The UN is Corrupt*: Consider the Iraqi Oil for food scandal. Also the sex for food scandal wherein peacekeepers were abusing women and children in exchange for food.

2. *The UN is Incompetent*: The UN can't account for more than one billion dollar shortfalls in both 2009 and 2010. There is no accurate accounting system, and further, no plans to introduce one.

3. *The UN is Anti-American*: The UN General Assembly is not able to agree on a definition of *terrorism* but continues to condemn the United States for bogus claims for Human Rights Violations.

4. *The UN is Ungrateful*: The US is by far the largest contributor to charitable projects administered by the UN, especially in sub-Saharan Africa and the Middle East. This generosity is totally unreturned. Intemperate speeches in the UN against the US are wildly applauded and countries that receive the most money from the US have even declared Holy War on us.

5. *The UN Costs Too Much*: *China*, which has 2.6 Trillion dollars in foreign exchange reserve contributes 4 percent of the UN Budget; India with billions of dollars in reserve, contributes 0.1 percent while the US contributes 22 percent or 568 Million Dollars in FY 2012 to the UN.

6. *The UN is Eroding American Sovereignty*: See the preceding sections.

7. *The UN wants to be The World Government*: See the preceding sections.[61]

Take Action Now

Reread the first section of this chapter. We are closer to this United Nation takeover than you might believe. If we intend to protect American sovereignty, we have no time to lose. You must appeal to your government representatives of both Houses to vote against ratification of any UN treaty. If they win, we are lost!

To recover from this will require a long and costly war against the UN forces. Anyone who fights against them and is taken prisoner must face the International Criminal Court, where a single malicious lie can cause you to be railroaded and incarcerated in a foreign prison, where you will very shortly and thoroughly understand just what rights you have lost. Assail Washington with all the e-mails, letters, phone calls, and other communications you can muster, to be certain that your representatives understand your position.

Regardless of who the next president is and regardless of which party is in power, we must monitor them carefully to make certain that they are responsive to the needs of the American people and to the two documents that constitute the power of the United States of America. We must ascertain correctly that they harbor no notions of one-world government. We must all stand firmly opposed to increased government growth and private perks for members of the Congress and the Senate. We must bond firmly together so that this problem, which we are now living through, does not survive and the United States of America does—as the country it was formed to be, for the benefit of all its citizens.

We must also accomplish something more difficult; we must be certain that all Americans pull together and none grow to expect unequal rights or equal results without equal effort. As Ben Franklin stated, "Yes, we must, indeed all hang together or, most assuredly, we shall all hang separately."[62] It is as true now as when he said it.

Chapter 7

Immigration

"If there is a country in the world where concord, according to common calculation, would be least expected, it is America. Made up as it is of people from different nations, accustomed to different forms and habits of government, speaking different languages, and more different in their modes of worship, it would appear that the union of such a people was impracticable; but by the simple operation of constructing government on the principles of society and the rights of man, every difficulty retires, and all the parts are brought into cordial unison."

Thomas Paine

America was lucky. There were no immigration requirements when relatively large number of immigrants began to arrive. England thought that she was getting rid of the riff-raff and the criminally inclined poor of the British Isles. Little did she realize what was actually happening under her nose.

A country can grow in two different ways, one of which is cataclysmic. An example is the formation of a country by virtue of a common cause, such as a war for independence. In this case, the common cause that bonds the people into a single aggregate is war, the nature of which causes the formation of goodwill. Because of fighting side by side and shoulder to shoulder, bonds of goodwill are formed between apparently very dissimilar factions. After fighting this way for an extensive period, very little thought is given to the dissimilarities that exist between brothers and sisters.

In fact, in the United States Revolutionary War, even though there were a relatively large number of loyalists, or Tories, in the colonies at that time, the fact that the country was largely united by the war led to this bonding. The Wikipedia entry on immigration is an interesting history updated through 2010 and composed of detailed facts and interesting statistics. References are provided for all statements.[63]

Immigration Requirements

As time passed, the governments that led the unprecedented growth of this country began to give thought to how they might serve the cause of immigration as well as the future protection of the country by establishing rules and regulations about immigration. The first regulations were passed in 1790. Immigration law is a complicated and sometimes incomprehensible set of rules and regulations and is beyond the scope of this work. Nevertheless, I will comment briefly on the issue.

First, there are essentially two methods of legitimate entry into the United States: with a visa or with a green card, which is proof of permanent resident status. Neither of these methods involves the process of naturalization, about which I will comment later.

There are over ten different types of visas, from a tourist visa to an application for citizenship. While the Homeland Security Act of 2002 complicated some regulations, it relaxed others and established new divisions under the umbrella of the newly commissioned Department of Homeland Security (DHS). Given the dangers of terrorist activity both inside and outside the United States, we are forced to wonder whether there is sufficient regulatory oversight of visas. The Homeland Security Act, has mandated extended wait times for Tourist visas and it is unclear whether all other types of entry documents are similarly restricted. This certainly warrants scrutiny.

Naturalization Requirements

Let's continue to explore the impact of extending the population of a country. The second way a country grows is relatively small in nature, even when accompanied by migrations of several thousand people of a common origin. In this case, the bonding of brothers and sisters becomes a more tenuous proposition. The greater the number of immigrants, the more likely it is that these immigrants will form into enclaves that share the same characteristics. The immigrating generation requires more time to join with the currently resident population. But the second generation of those immigrants joins society much quicker than its predecessor. For these first or later generations who desire to apply for citizenship (undergo naturalization), the requirements are as follows:

1. You already have a green card.
2. You are at least 18 years old.
3. You have lived in the United States lawfully as a permanent resident for at least five years *unless* you are a spouse of a United States citizen, refugee, or received your green card through political asylum.
4. During those five years, you have been physically present in the United States for at least half of the time.
5. You have not spent more than one year at a time outside the US.

6. You have not established a primary home in another country.

7. You have lived in the state or district where you are filing your application for at least three months.

8. You have "good moral character."

9. You can read, write, speak, and understand English.

10. You can pass a test about US history and government.

11. You will swear that you believe in the principles of the United States Constitution and will be loyal to the United States. [64]

12. **You will hold no other law above the Constitution of the United States and the associated laws of the United States and those of each individual state.** *(I have added this as a desired requirement.)*

If administered properly, these requirements are a remarkably good set of statutes. On the other hand, if they are not followed closely, they will destroy the very possibility that the new citizen will become a useful member of his or her new home.

For example, failure to demonstrate facility with the new language, English, should be cause for refusal to grant citizenship until a retest is passed. Facility with English, at least at the level of an eight- to twelve-year-old, is probably necessary for the ability to join the new culture. This is not meant to be a deterrent, but rather, to ensure the new citizen's ability to be productive in his or her new home. If English is not learned to this level, the new "citizen" will require all communication in his or her native tongue.

America is an English-speaking country, and no deviation from this should be permitted. The cost of providing multilingual documents is annually in excess of two billion dollars in the United States.[65] In these times, given the financial budgets issues we are facing, this amount of money should not be spent in such a flagrant manner.

There are numerous opportunities to learn English at the level required and at minimal or no cost. All people who cannot speak English at the fourth- to eighth-grade level should avail themselves of this opportunity. As things now stand, those persons may still live here, but they will not be true members of the country in which they live until they can speak its language.

Likewise, failure to establish a background free from violent or antisocial criminal activity, to prove good moral character, and to have a willingness to swear fealty to the US Constitution to the exclusion of the laws of all other countries should be cause for refusal to grant citizenship.

Surprisingly, the test for proficiency in English may be waived if the candidate fits within an exempted category or is over fifty. I view this waiver as a clear abortion of the intentions of the requirements, and it is neither in the best interests of the candidate nor of the United States. This is an area where it is important to appeal to your congressional representatives and senators to press for these enhanced changes to the naturalization requirements.

Difficulties of Immigration

The more the number of immigrants whose requirements of the new country differ significantly from the previously resident people increases, the less likely it is that we will join together at all. Indeed, it may be that the nature of their immigrating keeps them from ever becoming a cohesive part of the new country. Obviously, this condition is such that the nature of the welcoming country is forever changed, often not for the better.

It is difficult to see the immigrating masses being willing to contribute to the welfare of the previously resident people who differ so much from the immigrants themselves. Because of this, there is likely to be a gross refusal to do so, which may ultimately result in civil disorder. When this is carried to extremes, it may even result in civil war. Between the points of civil disorder and civil warfare lies a relatively long period, during which an increasing number of immigrants tends to take over the nature of the welcoming country until it bears little resemblance to its original state. This situation may be reasonably viewed as being unwelcome.

What started as an attempt to save the increasingly socialist nature of the country will lead to further decay from which no remedy is possible. Thus, this latter path to nation building is less desirable than the others, and any nation facing this is well advised to consider the options carefully. The following section on immigration deals with these and other problems created by poorly thought-out immigration policies

Immigration Dangers

Before I begin this section on immigration dangers, I would like to preface those remarks with this caveat: I have no ill will or animosity toward Muslim immigrants who are truly nonviolent and seek only to live under the freedoms granted to all Americans. Americans, in general, will welcome you if you truly come here without ulterior motive, without any desire to foment violence of any sort, and without any desire to implement Sharia law or any law contrary to the Constitution.

It's difficult to discuss this issue without pointedly considering that some immigrants attempt to bring their own legal system with them. It's clear that of all groups of immigrants, to my knowledge, only Muslims insist on practicing their form of legal system, Sharia law. This may not be true of all Muslim immigrants, e.g., it is known that some Muslims immigrate to escape Sharia. Perhaps it is a peculiarity of the violence-prone sects that abound. In any case, Sharia law can become a real danger, given the number of activist judges in America and, indeed, even those who have been bitten by the the one-world law sickness bug (see chapter six). Our Constitution guarantees each individual an equal set of rights, regardless of race, gender, or religion. Because of this, Sharia law is itself unconstitutional and incompatible with the rule of law in our constitutional republic.

The Council on American and Islamic Relations (CAIR), a terrorist-linked organization, has launched a media offensive that deems anyone who questions Islam in America or who is concerned about a recurrence of the 9/11 attacks, as Islamophobic. According to Lisa Gardiner, reporting in the San Ramon Valley Herald, Omar Ahmad, cofounder and former chairman of CAIR, made the following statement in a speech: "Islam isn't in America to be equal to any other faith, but to become dominant. The Koran, the Muslim book of Scripture should be the highest authority in America, and Islam the only accepted religion on earth."[66]

In spite of this blatant example of attempting to supplant the Constitution and the rule of law in this country, no attempt has been made to correct this and similar statements made by Islamic organizations. President Obama has officially recognized the Muslim Brotherhood as a legitimate organization, while declaring Israel a supporter of terrorism.

This can only be stopped by becoming familiar with the Islamic threat and writing to your representatives as soon as possible.

Sharia law is contrary to basic human rights and cannot be allowed to supplant the Constitution or to complicate the American judicial system. Only *your voice* against this powerful enemy can stop its progress.

Because of this danger to the United States, all persons seeking a permanent residence visa or naturalization should be made to comply with the requirement twelve in the amended list of naturalization requirements earlier in this chapter. If persons seeking the above forms of immigration refuse to attest to requirement twelve, they should be refused residence in the United States. Legislation pertaining to this must be pursued with both branches of Congress. Once again, only your voice can command it.

Illegal Immigration

The undocumented immigrant population in the United States has been estimated by the Center for Immigration Studies to be about eleven million people. Additional estimates range from seven to twenty million people.[67] The vast majority of illegal aliens enter across the US-Mexico border. This border is partially fenced and is supposed to be guarded by the US Border Patrol, an organization responsible to the Department of Homeland Security. The Border Patrol is an exhausted, overworked, and unsupported (by their high-level supervisors) organization.

It should not be surprising that as illegal aliens cross this border, they introduce violence, crime, and disease. Tuberculosis, dysentery, typhoid, malaria, tapeworm, river blindness, and guinea worm have been documented as having been associated with illegal aliens.[68] The following statistics should grasp your attention:

- 113 billion dollars is this year's cost of illegal immigration. Approximately 75 percent of this amount is absorbed by the states.
- $1,117 is the average amount you and your family paid in taxes to support illegals.
- 52 billion dollars is the annual cost of educating children of illegals.
- $2,700 is the average dollar amount a single illegal household costs the government.
- 51 percent of Mexican immigrant households use at least one major welfare program and 28 percent use more than one.
- 1.4 million illegal immigrant households use at least one major welfare program. (These include Food Stamps, WIC, school lunch, Medicaid, TANF, SSI and public, rent-subsidized housing.)[69]

As if this were not enough, President Obama seeks to bypass the legislative process by means of executive policy to grant amnesty for the twelve to twenty million illegal aliens that currently reside in the United States. This is set forth in a memorandum entitled "Administrative Alternatives to Comprehensive Immigration Reform." According to World Net Daily, this memo is a blueprint for a presidential dictatorship.[70]

Janet Napolitano, secretary of the DHS, is wasting her efforts and government money in seeking to categorize illegal aliens who will not be deported at all. The Obama administration has already instructed Immigration and Customs Enforcement (ICE) to stop deporting many illegal aliens.[71] All of this is part of a poorly concealed plan to suborn the 2012 election by placing more than thirty million votes from the pro-amnesty forces in the Obama column.

This is an out-and-out abuse of executive power and the office of the president. Is there any question what will happen after this becomes a reality? Can anyone explain the effect of adding untold millions of once-illegal aliens to the welfare rolls in this country? This administration will not be satisfied until it has reduced this once-great country to a has-been and has discarded it on the trash heap of history. God help us all!

How blind can the minions of the Democratic Party be? By mustering all the kindness possible, one attempts to excuse their errant behavior as humanitarian in origin. My friends in Texas would say, "That dog won't hunt!" How, then, do they excuse the flagrant violence done to women, young and older, as well as youngsters? There are significant dangers associated with illegal immigration. This also includes potential death while crossing the border. For example,

- Operation Gatekeeper has forced illegals to traverse more dangerous routes to get into the United States.
- Many die of dehydration in the heat of the Arizona desert.
- Some die while resisting arrest.
- Numerous foreign women are brought into Mexico under false pretenses, smuggled across the US border and forced to work as prostitutes, sweatshop laborers, and farmhands.
- Some women trafficked into the United States have often been forced to have sex with as many as five hundred men to pay off their passage debt of forty thousand dollars.
- Each year, at least forty-five thousand Central American children attempt to immigrate illegally, and many of them end up as sex slaves.
- Many migrants are killed or maimed when riding the roofs of cargo trains in Mexico.

This is where misguided pity takes you—to the unspeakable crimes perpetrated on these innocents. Give it up, and place your pity where it should lie. Realize where the American democracy will be when twenty-odd million more souls are on the public dole and the country begins to sink under the weight of these poor hangers-on.

Then ask yourself who instigated these socialist programs? Who caused all these people, who were also due dignity, to fall short, to fail to achieve even the least bit of the American Dream? Those who see where we will be taken by misguided amnesty should ring the phones off the hooks in our Capitol; cause the mail to your representatives to be delivered in cartons and your e-mails to slow down all the computer systems in D.C. as well. This is not a selfish rant by persons consumed by greed. This is a cry for justice for all.

Chapter 8

Other Political Problems

"Government, like dress, is the badge of lost innocence."

Thomas Paine

Several issues are covered in this chapter, but this does not imply that they have lesser importance than other issues in this book. Indeed, many of these issues are of major importance, but they require less explanation than others. There also is no significance to the order of issues in this chapter.

How the Democratic Party Secures Votes

Association of the Democrats with Unions: One of the methods by which the Democratic Party has long secured additional large blocks of votes is through its leaders cozying up to various unions. The old adage "Follow the money" is applicable here. Matthew Boyle recently published a list of unions and their contributions to the Democratic Party in the 2008 and 2010 elections.[72] These contributions do not include any money spent directly by the unions on behalf of the Democratic Party and/or specific candidates for various offices, such as television and newspaper ads. Thirteen unions contributed 31.2 million dollars to the 2008 elections campaign and 27.5 million dollars to the 2010 election campaign. Only extremely small percentages of these amounts ever reached the coffers of the Republican Party from the same sources.

The majority of the members of these unions cannot possibly be Democrat to the extent that the contributions of the union reflect. For example, usually between 90 to 95 percent of union contributions are tendered to the Democratic Party. The National Education Association (NEA) contributed 2.3 million dollar in 2008 and 2.2 million in 2010. The American Federation of Teachers (AFT), on the other hand, contributed 2.8 million dollars in 2008 and 2.7 million in 2010.

It is difficult not to speculate on the reason for this close association. Apparently, the unions are closely bound to the organizations that the unions represent. This would seem to be a case of one hand washing the other. In other words, the unions extend money largely to the Democratic Party. In the *sotto voce* agreement that takes place, the party agrees to support legislation that the union wishes to see passed.

Also, the members of the union are strongly encouraged to vote for the party that passes their desired legislation. Obviously, it's impossible to control the voting of individual union members, but the association works for the benefit of both. So it seems that this situation exists between the unions and the Democratic Party. In other words, the union is buying votes from the party in exchange for votes in favor of the political party at the election booth. Of course, this is hard to prove, but it's plausible.

Association of the Democrats with Large Organizations: The situation here is analogous to that with the Democratic Party and unions. In fact, any large organization that can muster a large number of votes is in essentially the same situation. This is especially true with minority groups. The Democrats are quick to say whatever the minority wants to hear; and in that fashion controls that block of votes. Of course, in exchange, the political party agrees to support the causes of the minority group. Naturally, both parties are eager and willing to cozy up with any organization with which they share philosophies.

On the other hand, it seems clear that the largest amounts of money go to the Democratic Party. For example, the well-known multibillionaires George Soros and Warren Buffett clearly support the Democratic Party almost to the exclusion of all others for the most part. Whether they do this by direct contribution or through the formation of front corporations, we may never know. In any case, they can contribute incredible amounts of money to so-called Super PACS.

This not only provides large amounts of money that can be used for radio and television advertising, but also gives the candidates an opportunity by which they can deny any attachment to the Super Pac, which is providing the cash for the advertising. In this fashion, the candidates can say what they really want to say and yet at the same time can plausibly deny that they had any knowledge of the content of the ad. This can also be applied to the Republican Party, but if you follow the large amounts of money, you almost always end up at or near the Democratic Party.

As discussed in the previous chapter, President Obama's plan for circumventing the legislature and offering backdoor amnesty by means of executive action is clearly intended to garner an additional twelve to twenty million votes for a second term as president. This must be prevented by any legal means possible.

Association of the Democrats with Community Organizers:
When properly administered, a community organization is an
acceptable way to accomplish many useful actions. But when
it's run in the Saul Alinsky manner, every method—legal and
otherwise—is brought into play, including false registration
and nonregistration, multiple voting by the same individual,
and intimidation by the strong-arm thugs at the polling places,
especially those frequented by older citizens.

Barack Obama has long been associated with community
organizers and is reputed to have been trained in the Alinsky
method. Obama's first mentor, Mike Kruglik, says that he was
"the best student he ever had."[73] He was a natural, the undisputed
master of agitation. Obama has had a long and intimate
association with the Association of Community Organizations
for Reform Now (ACORN), the largest radical group in the
United States.[74]

ACORN is the key modern successor of the 1960s New Left, which
grew out of the National Welfare Rights Organization (NWRO),
one of the New Left's most destructive groups, which led a
campaign of sit-ins and disruptions at welfare offices. Their goal
was to flood welfare rolls with enough clients to break the system
by removing eligibility restrictions. Instead of a socialist utopia,
we inherited a culture of dependency and family breakdown
until welfare reform began to turn the tide.

Fast-forward to the early years of the new millennium, and ACORN retains the economic framework of NWRO and its confrontational tactics. According to Sol Stern,

> ACORN's bedrock assumption remains the ultra-Left's anti-capitalist redistributionism...At times, ACORN opts for undisguised authoritarian socialism, as when it proposes that "large companies which desire to leave the community" be forced to obtain "an exit visa from the community board signifying that the company has adequately compensated all its employees and the community at large for losses due to relocation." How much longer before acorn calls for exit visas for wealthy or middle-class individuals before they can leave the city? This is the road to serfdom indeed, even though it begins with little steps...There may be different approaches to community organizing. But there should also be a community organizer's version of the oath of Hippocrates: "First, do no harm." [75]

The leopard has not changed its spots. ACORN remains the same anticapitalist, socialist-leaning organization unopposed to bullying, intimidation, and criminal activities, as previously reported. The Democrats are guilty of misleading the inner-city poor, bleeding them of their votes and ignoring on dual voting and voting by the dead. They would do well to learn that "you are who and what your friends are."

Further, they would do wisely to follow Mark 9:41: "And whosoever shall lead one of these little ones astray, it were better for him that a millstone be hung about his neck and he be cast into the sea." Those who mislead the poor are certainly leading them astray. The end does not justify the means. Further stories of illegal activity at the polls are given in reference.[76]

The Constitutionality of ObamaCare

At this time, ObamaCare remains to be defeated. Several cases have been brought before the individual appellate courts, and it has been both defended and attacked by individual federal judges. The Supreme Court has finally agreed to hear the case in the spring of 2012. The Committee for Justice (CFJ) is a public-interest law center whose mission is to restore limited constitutional government in America. The CFJ does this

> by helping Americans defend their constitutional rights when they come under attack from our own government—such as with ObamaCare, the most misguided and dangerous law ever enacted in the history of the United States...The Constitutions "commerce clause" grants Congress power to regulate interstate economic activity.

But the Obama administration is actually claiming that this section of the Constitution also grants Congress power to force citizens to purchase products—including health insurance.

Never before in our nation's history has any administration attempted to claim this power. Nor has any court ever ruled that economic activity includes economic inactivity, such as the decision not to buy health insurance—which is what the Obama Justice Department is claiming.

Under this novel interpretation of Congress' power to regulate economic activity, federal government power becomes virtually unlimited.[77]

The CFJ has filed an *amicus curiae* brief in support of Florida and twenty-five other states, resulting from its conclusion that ObamaCare is unconstitutional. The main arguments are as follows:

1. The individual mandate is unconstitutional because it exceeds Congress's power under the commerce clause.
2. The individual mandate is unconstitutional because it is not a tax and thus does not fall under Congress's power to tax
3. The act violates the Tenth Amendment of the Constitution by trespassing on the sovereignty of the states.

4. The entire act must be struck down because the unconstitutional individual mandate is not severable from the rest of the act.

Each of the above four arguments is supported by several subordinate arguments. If you have not received any information about the pending attempt to declare ObamaCare unconstitutional, contact the Committee for Justice and request the Honorary Citizen Plaintiff's Petition and associated material.

The Recusal of Justice Elena Kagan

[As of this writing, the Supreme Court has taken up the case, and Justice Kagan has not recused herself. Nevertheless, I am allowing this section to remain in place to ensure that readers may have the opportunity to review this matter.]

It appears obvious that President Obama had assumed that this law would be questioned, possibly by the United States Supreme Court. Accordingly, he appointed Elena Kagan, who was then solicitor general and who would later be named to the Supreme Court, to prepare a defense for this pending legislation. Even though Kagan, now a Supreme Court justice, is legally required to recuse herself or face possible impeachment, she has not done so. The Kagan ObamaCare Recusal Task Force, a special project of the Traditional Values Coalition (TVC),[78] is bringing pressure to bear on the Justice Department, Kagan, and the Obama administration. Kagan has personally recused herself in twenty-nine other cases, but she still refuses to do so in this case:

> Federal law 28 U.S.C. Section 455(a) requires that a justice recuse himself "in any proceeding in which his impartiality might reasonably be questioned" or any time he has "expressed an opinion concerning the merits of a particular case in controversy" while serving in "governmental employment."[78]

The Recusal Task Force has deliberated on ten issues concerning then-Solicitor General Kagan that demonstrated recusal was warranted. At that point, the task force concluded,

> Elena Kagan cannot impartially judge legal arguments about a law which she herself helped craft before it was even passed, and for which she has shown such enthusiasm. The Justice Department knows that and will continue stonewalling and redacting crucial evidence.[78]

In view of this information, it seems clear that Kagan should recuse herself or be impeached and convicted, if necessary.[79]

The Energy Crisis

We have a leader who refuses to recognize the energy crisis in this country. To be sure, he pays it lip service, but he refuses to alienate the Environmental Protection Agency and the thousands of people who work for this overweight and grossly overbudgeted organization. The EPA also has its tens of thousands of followers who cannot seem to understand that people are the real species in danger in the world today. Of course, these people will be appeased by Obama's performance, and therefore many of them will vote for him in 2012.

Thousands of people are opposed to the Keystone XL pipeline and hydraulic fracturing ("fracking"), so whom do you think they will vote for? Obama was no doubt eyeing the upcoming election when he threw a bouquet to unhappy environmentalists by delaying a decision on the XL pipeline until after the vote.[80] Sol Sanders in his "Follow the Money" column had this to say:

> Scandal after scandal is proving that the Obama administration's so-called "green energy" strategy is corrupt, wasteful and ineffectual. Keystone, on the other hand, would put crude into the Texas Petrochemical refinery complex already absorbing similar but heavier oil from Venezuela, whose reserves were recently re-estimated upward with spectacular finds on the Orinoco River.[80]

In the meantime, the trade deficit has ballooned, causing the administration to have fits, since they have dictated certain positions, as central planners are wont to do. A few examples illustrate the chief central planner's lack of foresight and fixation on his pronouncements. The article "The Central Plan" in the March 5, 2012, issue of *National Review* [81] reads as follows:

So bothered by the trade deficit is President Obama that he seeks to impose his political will not only on the US economy but also on the Chinese economy demanding that Beijing revise its monetary policy and its trade rules to favor American exports. If they hadn't been paralyzed with laughter, the central planners in China might have pointed out to President Obama that the single largest contributor to the US trade deficit is not cheap Chinese manufactured goods but a single non-Chinese commodity: oil, which accounts for one half of the deficit. As it happens, the Obama administration has been busily undermining domestic energy production in the United States, because its central planning manifesto says that the US economy should cease to run on petroleum and begin to run on other forms of energy wind, hydro, geothermal, etc.[81]

The Marcellus Shale bed lies deep underground, extending from West Virginia to New York State. Below this shale bed, lies so much natural gas that the amount is usually written in scientific notation, such as 4.36×10^{14} cubic feet, or 436 trillion cubic feet, suggesting that there is enough gas to provide fifteen years of total US energy use there for the taking. Further, a recent report by Abby W. Schachter states that U.S. Government experts predict that there is more than 2.5 quadrillion cubic feet of recoverable natural gas in the entire country. This can be expected to provide for total domestic use including home and office heating and the clean generation of electrical energy. This is the amount that can be obtained by Hydraulic Fracturing or fracking, which will provide for the country's energy use for the next 95 years. Non-governmental experts say that there is enough natural gas to last for three times that long, not to mention the creation of enough so-called "shovel-ready jobs" for millions of workers. See endnote 82 referencing the June column by Abby W. Schachter in *Commentary Magazine.*

Since the Japanese nuclear accident, the Japanese have been ready to purchase incredible amounts of natural gas from anyone in the world. Since the fracking process is being used to extract the natural gas from eight thousand feet under the ground, it is to be expected that the EPA will take its heavy-handed approach in this as well, resulting in an increased deficit as has happened with the Keystone XL project as well.

As it is, the EPA has already issued a draft report that charges that fracking is responsible for the pollution of drinking water in Pavillion, Wyoming. In a news report by Ben Wolfgang, the following statement was made:

> A highly critical report from the agency likely would stir greater opposition to fracking and could deal a major blow to one of the few economic success stories of the past few years.

> "It becomes harder and harder to believe that [increased natural gas production] is what the president wishes to happen" said John Engler, president of the Business Roundtable, in an interview with *Washington Times* editors and reporters...EPA made mistakes and misjudgments at almost every step of the process...Many of EPA's findings are conjecture, not fact, and only serve to trigger undue alarm.[82]

The EPA has indeed become a ruthless juggernaut, riding roughshod over legitimate enterprise, just as it did when it decided to classify milk as "an oil."[83] Never mind that the EPA found in a 2004 study that hydraulic fracturing, (fracking) did not present any danger to human health and the environment. However, that was Bush's EPA. Do we really need to spend another two million dollars to restudy the process?

A study conducted by HIS Global Insight estimates that a ban on fracking would cost the United States 374 billion dollars in lost GDP as well as about three million jobs. It would also require us to import an additional 60 percent of oil and natural gas. To advance their agenda, the EPA and its followers are playing a game in which the smallest risks are turned into the biggest threats.[84]

A March 13, 2012 article in the *Wall Street Journal* [85] reported that faulty wells, rather than fracking, are the cause of gas seepage into the water table. An additional pipe barrier as well as additional cement casing of the pipe lining has proven that fracking is a safe procedure.

Cost of ObamaCare

[This case is currently before the Supreme Court and may be decided prior to publication of this book. As it stands, the individual mandate is certain to be judged as unconstitutional. Given that there is no severability clause, we would guess that ObamaCare is deader than a doornail. However, as we have seen in the past, anything can happen.]

Another example of presidental stonewalling is the Patient Protection and Affordable Care Act (PPACA). Based on the data that tells us that 45.7 million Americans are uninsured, PPACA was implemented. Keith Hennesey, the former director of the National Economic Council, calculated the actual number of uninsured Americans as 10.6 million; the remaining "uninsured" included many who were *not* truly uninsured, another large number who were not Americans (because noncitizens were also counted), and another group who chose to be uninsured. The report went on to say:

> The average cost for an insurance policy for a single person in 2011 was $5429, meaning that we could have bought insurance for all those uninsured (10.6 million) for about 58 billion dollars a year. The Obama administration says the PPACA will cost about 93 billion per year, not quite twice what it would cost them just to buy people insurance, whereas former Congressional Budget Office director Douglas Holtz-Eakin calculates that the program will end up costing about $893 billion a year or 15 times what it would cost to just buy people insurance.[86]

Both of the previous sections illustrate how poorly planned the plans are. In true socialist style, once a plan is formulated, no power on earth, including correcting the input data, is allowed to topple the plan.

President Obama's 2013 Budget

According to Obama,[87] the new 2013 budget will "restore an economy where everybody gets a fair shot." This is to be done by implementing an estimated 3.8-trillion-dollar election-year budget. In an in-your-face proposal, the president called for short-term spending with proposals already rejected by the

GOP lawmakers. This is where a line item veto given both to the legislature and to the president is warranted. Some of the items included are:

1. Thirty billion dollars to hire teachers and emergency workers. *This can be corrected by Solution A below.*

2. Fifty billion dollars on transportation infrastructures. *Solution A*

3. Thirty billion dollars to modernize schools. Solution A

4. Extension of the payroll tax holiday through FY 2012, already approved. *No change.*

5. A 30 percent minimum tax on those earning one million dollars or more. *Delete, since these people will do the investing that produces jobs. Solution B.*

6. Raise taxes on investment income on those families earning over 250,000 dollars. *Delete. Solution C.*

7. Tax dividends as ordinary income, raising the top bracket from 15 percent to 39.6 percent. *Delete. See Solution B.*

8. Capital gains income for the top-income bracket would rise from 15 percent to 30 percent. *Solution B. How many times do we have to relearn this?*

9. Do nothing to address the 15.3 trillion dollars national debt. *Strike and replace with a reasonable proposal.*

10. Borrow a total of 901 billion. *Reduce to as low as possible.*

11. Obama's ten-year plan would add 11.2 trillion dollars to the national debt. *Reduce to as low as possible.*

12. Retain 1.3 billion dollars in aid to Egypt. *Delete until American democracy activists are released. Reinstate at no more than 10 percent of original.*

13. New 770 million dollars in the Middle East and North Africa to promote democracy. *See number 12.* For information on the solutions, please see the section following the comments below.

Comments worth considering: [88]

- Senator Jeff Sessions, (R—AL: "It's a tax and spend budget virtually identical to the path we are currently on…Where is the $4 trillion in deficit reduction?"

- David A. Walker, former US comptroller general: "The president's budget fails to lay out a substantive path to restore fiscal sanity.

- Senator Mark Pryor, (D–AK): "I am concerned that spending on luxury items, such as high speed rail and spaceship taxis, takes preference over basic needs. I will not support a budget that sidelines basic needs…and still results in a whopping $770 billion deficit in 2022."

Explanations of Solutions:

Solution A: Organize into four groups by numeric and urgency categories. Implement one-quarter of each group each year, making allowances for size, need to complete, and so on.

Solution B: This is counterproductive. The contributions and investment by this group predominantly funds jobs. How long before this president and the Democrats learn that these Neo-Keynesian economic policies are the path to serfdom?

You can force these changes by writing to your senators and congresspeople and advising them that we are opposed to Obama's 2013 budget. Don't let the opportunity slip by. Delay will hurt no one but our families and ourselves. The only way to recover our S&P bond rating is to demonstrate strongly our commitment to accomplish this.

Reduction of Big Government

Every year, we get several mega-doses of congressional claptrap about reducing big government. If it's an election year, this becomes giga-doses from the candidates for either election or reelection. And every year, when the smoke clears, we find that the size of government has increased.

It's high time that we insisted that legislation be crafted and enacted, *not* buried in committee for endless months. It's time for us to demand that government be reduced by not less than 2 percent each year. This way, we can be assured that twenty years will produce a sizeable reduction in the government workforce.

In addition, every time one of the branches of Congress passes a rule or regulation, or law that requires the addition of personnel to the current workforce, those additional personnel *must* be taken from other programs or offices, or from other shadow personnel, so that net growth is zero. This reduction doesn't count toward the mandated 2 percent annual reduction. This may not be amended or modified in any manner inconsistent with the intent of this proposed law.

After the usual congressional growth hormones are applied to the above paragraph, it should grow to the typical one hundred or so pages of governmental subterfuge, legerdemain, and trickery, in which enough methods are provided to undo the intent of the above paragraph. Hence the last few sentences.

In addition, after forcing a vote on this issue, the roll call of the vote shall be published in every major newspaper in the appropriate districts or state. A legislator who votes against this proposal should be threatened by recall and expulsion from Congress by his or her constituents.

Chapter 9

January 30, 1933, Redux

"Arms discourage and keep the invader and plunderer in awe, and preserve order in the world as well as property...Horrid mischief would ensue were the law-abiding deprived of the use of them."

Thomas Paine

For those who have forgotten their history or perhaps are too young to know, January 30, 1933, the birthday of the Third Reich,[89] the government that savaged the world under the leadership of the demagogue Adolf Hitler. Four things point in this direction.

The first step in undermining democracy is gun control, by which means a people are enslaved and rendered helpless in the face of an army controlled by a megalomaniac. The second step is giving the impression of an unwillingness to defend oneself. The third is identity papers or a national identity card. And fourth is the militarization of the home front.[90] The final three impositions are easily implemented once the first is brought into being.

The Insanity of Gun Control

The issue of gun control warrants a chapter of its own. But because it fits so closely with the others in this chapter, I will deal with it here. In spite of what most people think, self-protection is not granted by the United States Constitution or any state constitution. It is a God-given right, and the Constitution merely gives it legal presence. There is a natural law instituted by God to enable His creatures to protect themselves. Therefore, anyone who, by the passage of bills or laws contrary to natural law, attempts to remove your ability to protect yourself or your family without just cause, places citizens in an untenable position. In doing so, they place themselves in the role of an unjust aggressor. All upright citizens are justified in protecting themselves by any means available.

Notwithstanding the two recent Supreme Court decisions finding that the Second Amendment guarantees an individual right, Obama, his Justice Department (Eric Holder, of "Fast and Furious" fame), and his State Department (Hillary Clinton) have not curtailed their plans to enact major antigun legislation. The UN plan mentioned in the chapter on US sovereignty, while contrary to the US Constitution, will not withstand the assault by the United Nations if the seventeen treaties Obama wants passed become reality, since UN law would replace the Constitution. It has already been demonstrated that our government does not respect natural law.

Several papers or news articles have been written that bear on this issue. The first article, entitled "Holder tells Congress the Obama administration wants to ban guns"[91] appeared in the *Daily Caller*. Attorney General Eric Holder is quoted as saying,

> This administration has consistently favored the reinstitution of the assault weapons ban. It is something that we think was useful in the past with regard to the reduction we have seen in crime, and certainly would have a positive impact on our relationship and the crime situation in Mexico.[92]

The absolute lack of logic in this statement is mind-boggling. (See the section "Greed and Fraud" for a discussion of Operation "Fast and Furious"; also see the endnote[92].) This incredible scandal was overseen by our own Justice Department (or higher authority), which allowed over 2,500 illegally purchased guns to be "walked" into Mexico, resulting in the death of US Border Patrol Agent Brian Terry.

Holder claims that he does not know how, why, or who caused this scandal. He also refuses to allow an astonishingly large number of internal documents to be turned to the congressional committee looking into this debacle. Because of this, Obama and Holder seem to believe that banning a large number of legal firearms from US citizens who use these every day for legal activities will somehow solve the Mexican crime problem.

It has been repeatedly proven that, in this country, the widespread availability of firearms has consistently decreased the occurrence of violent crime.[93] Anyone who can read and is willing to do so, can determine this. That both Obama and Holder appear to be ignorant of the facts seems to indicate an unwillingness to acquaint themselves with the substantiated matter. Indeed, it seems that both would rather portray themselves as illiterate than accept the peer-reviewed research of countless social scientists and legal professionals.

Neither of these politicians seems able to appreciate that this is not a Republican, Democratic, or Mexican issue. It's an American issue, and all Americans need to understand why the US Supreme Court and the Constitution are subject to the whims of bureaucratic politicians. It's time to admit that America made a gem of a mistake when it elected Obama, and we must not let it happen again. Obama has decided that he is the person who decides which laws must be obeyed. He has said,

> I have advised Congress that I will not construe these provisions as preventing me from fulfilling my constitutional responsibility to recommend to the Congress's [sic] consideration such measures as I shall judge necessary and expedient.[94]

Another paper, "The Arms Trade Treaty (ATT) and Our Constitution's Loophole," is several pages long but bears close reading.[95] A short synopsis is that the loophole in the US Constitution is in article two, section two, which states, "He [the president] shall have Power, by and with the Advice and Consent of the Senate, to make treaties, provided two thirds of the Senators present concur."

[People, in general, seem to be put off by extended quotes, perhaps assuming that the author will clarify the information contained therein. In this case, the arguments put forth are both complicated and subtle, and it is imperative to take the bull by the horns and to persevere in reading this information.]

The author of *The Second Amendment and Gun Control*, Joseph Bruce Alonso, states:

> In the United States, acceptance of a treaty is ratification by the Senate. By signing, a sovereign state does indicate an intention to ratify or at least consider and abide by a treaty... if a treaty conflicts with the United States Constitution, United States Supreme Court will hold that the treaty is not binding because it violates the United States Constitution. If the same conflict came before an international court, the international court would hold that the treaty was binding. These competing legal systems are on a road to conflict... The United States Constitution clearly anticipates the United States federal government entering into treaties but does not appear to have anticipated the extent to which treaties would have domestic ramifications... The desire to end all private gun ownership world-wide is a final goal of many international law actors. This desire is often hidden or lightly shrouded, but is sometimes flaunted... Based on the intensity of disapproval aimed at the United States, one expects... politics will push in the direction... to end private gun ownership...The ways in which the rights of private United States gun owners could be infringed are endless. Clearly, a final goal of eliminating private gun ownership [the UN's agenda] would violate

the Second Amendment...The first way is the possibility that the president of the United States signs [a treaty]... Signature by the United States President would indicate to the international community that the United States intends to abide by the gun control laws, with or without ratification by the Senate.[96]

That final phrase says that the act of the president alone can obviate the requirement of a two-third majority vote of the Senate. This would subject the United States and the rest of the world to disarmament. In a paper by David Kopel, et al., entitled "The Human Right of Self-Defense,"[97] we find the following:

While it is unlikely that a severely restrictive international gun control treaty could be ratified by two thirds of the United States Senate, there are many mechanisms by which unratified treaties can work their way into U. S. law. For example some eminent international disarmament experts have taken the position that the president of the United States may announce that a treaty has entered into force and thereby becomes the law of the United States even if the United States Senate has never voted to ratify the treaty. The United States Supreme Court has cited unratified treaties (and even an African treaty), and various contemporary foreign law sources, as guidance for interpreting United States constitutional provisions. Likewise other scholars writing in a UN publication, argue that United Nations gun control documents (notwithstanding the fact that the documents, on their face, have no binding legal effect) represent *"norms"* of international law.[98]

The final paragraph in the Gallant paper is startling: "That means you—or any of us—could be prosecuted by an international court *with all our protections asserted in the Bill of Rights thrown down the proverbial drain."*[96]

This means that there is practically no hope that this issue can be resolved without war. Even if the United States clearly decides to remove itself from the United Nations (an act I strongly approve), we may face an international war against a task force hell-bent on forcing us under the supranational United Nations. The dangers are clear. *We cannot afford a man at the helm of this country who wants to be a "citizen of the world."*

Unilateral Disarmament

As if the previous was not enough to contend with, recent events reported in the news should cause all of us to fall to our knees in prayer.[98] Because of the simple mistake of a microphone left on, a conversation between President Obama and Russia's Dmitry Medvedev became, fortunately for us, public knowledge. After a meeting in South Korea, the president told Medvedev that he required "space" before he could talk with the Russians about missile defense negotiations. The "space" he was alluding to was presumably the need to put the 2012 presidential election behind him. In other words, the fear is that he would certainly lose the election if the results of those talks were made known before it, which certainly doesn't say much for the benefit of these discussions to the American people.

"After my election, I have more flexibility," Obama is reported to have told the Russian president.[99]

Medvedev is reported to have said, "Yes, I understand. I will tell Vladimir [Putin]."

Regarding this interchange, presidential hopeful Rick Santorum said, "This isn't about politics. This is about the president's real agenda...The president's real agenda is to withdraw and allow... the Russians or the Chinese or whoever it is, the Iranians, let them have their run of the table because America's no longer in the business of protecting ourselves and our allies."

Whether this is the president's real agenda is less important, perhaps, than his apparent contempt for American voters as well as for the Constitution of the United States, which he has sworn to protect and defend.

It's unconscionable to think about nuclear disarmament at a time when rogue nations such as North Korea and Iran are racing toward the ability to rain down nuclear holocaust on the

United States and her allies. Indeed, we don't even know how much materiel and guidance the Russians and/or the Chinese are providing to these countries in their hope to have the ability to leave America in the dust of either a race toward world dominance or a nuclear explosion. In any case, it's no longer possible to think of our president as an "America first" political leader. We are forced to wonder, in the final analysis, whom is he rooting for?

This is not solely this writer's opinion. US Representative Michael Turner and thirty-three other members of Congress recently wrote a letter [100] to the president, which said, in part,

> We seek your assurance that in view of the ambitious nuclear weapons modernization programs of Russia, communist China, Pakistan and others, the deep cuts in US conventional capabilities per the Budget Control Act and your failure to follow through on your pledged [modernization of the deterrent] that you will cease to pursue such unprecedented reductions in the US deterrent and extended deterrent. [101]

The legislators also pointed out that even if Obama was unable to achieve the sweeping reductions he has in mind, he can still accomplish America's unilateral disarmament. All that he needs to do is permit the continued atrophy of our increasingly obsolescent nuclear forces. Most of these weapon system components are greater than twenty-five years old and have not been realistically tested for over two decades. [As with matches, a 100 percent test is not useful. However, "realistic" in the preceeding sentence is intended to mean a statistically significant test is required.] Due to the impending election, the president is apparently unwilling to speak openly about the unknown additional nuclear defense reductions that were presumably communicated to Medvedev. One can only surmise that Obama thinks that speaking openly before the election is tantamount to allowing the opposing candidate to carry off the coming moment of truth, i.e. to win the election.

Can the president actually be trying to communicate to the world at large his unwillingness to fight? Can he possibly believe that a Gandhi-like posture is any sort of protection or deterrent in today's world? Is he trying to say that he will not defend Israel or come to its aid? Or is he saying that the game is getting too rough or that the United States no longer has the financial wherewithal to risk a major war? Of course, we are not exactly defenseless. Nevertheless, his secretiveness shows a lack of healthy respect for his citizenry and undermines their respect for him. In any case, we are forced to wonder if we dare to reelect him.

National Identity Cards

The thought of national ID cards brings fear to the average American, and the Internet is loaded with references to it.

Google "National ID Card," and I guarantee your screen will be covered with access to tens of millions entries from 2004 up to the present.[101-103]

Can the requirement of an ID card happen? Do we have a president who is above the law? He claims that he is.[104] If two Supreme Court decisions and article 2 of the Bill of Rights will not stop him, what will? As of this writing, it has not happened yet. But does that mean it will not happen tomorrow or next week or next year? Does this not suggest a legitimate course of action to you? And further, one you cannot trust to happen without coercion? If the United States is to be preserved, we must not only have a change of administration, but we must remain eternally vigilant that such actions may not occur.

Militarization of the Homefront

In a recent commentary, Joseph Farah, a nationally syndicated columnist suggested[105] that in July 2008, presidential candidate Barack Obama vowed to create a "civilian national security force that's just as powerful, just as strong, just as well-funded" as the US military. Two paragraphs later, the article said,

But two recent developments suggest Obama may have found an innovative way to achieve his objectives to militarize the homefront without creating a new national security force: in December (2011), both houses of Congress passed the Defense reauthorization bill that killed the concept of habeas corpus—legislation that authorized the president to use the US military to arrest and indefinitely detain American citizens without charge or trial.[106]

Citing that "there is no compelling military need for this change," Army General Martin Dempsey, chairman of the joint chiefs of staff, during his congressional testimony on the bill, spoke against the National Guard's top officer becoming the fifth member of the body that advises the president on national security matters. In fact, all six four-star generals constituting the joint chiefs testified in a November 10, 2011, hearing of the Senate Armed Forces Services Committee that the idea of including the National Guard chief as a member of the joint chiefs would create unneeded confusion and lessen the authority of the other military representatives.

Even Leon Panetta, Obama's personally chosen secretary of defense, opposed the measure. Further, Panetta told reporters that membership on the joint chiefs should "be reserved for those who have direct command and direct budgets that deal with the military." Farah went on to say,

The national security force Obama mused about in 2008 is in place. It's just not civilian, it's military. It's no longer a question of whether political dissidents are going to hear that dreaded knock on the door in America. It's only a question of who is going to have their door knocked down by US military forces and be dragged kicking and screaming to Guantánamo Bay without even the right to talk to an attorney.[106]

Interestingly, or perhaps fearfully, the media declined to pursue an explanation of what can only be described as a fundamental break from the Constitution's protection of individual rights and the long-held tradition of the US military being kept out of domestic civilian life. In addition, two four-star Marine generals Charles C. Krulak and Joseph P. Hoar, have written an opinion piece in the *New York Times*[106] demanding that President Obama veto the NDAA (HR 1540 and S 1867) to protect our country from "the false choice between our safety and ideals."

Let's remind ourselves of what Benjamin Franklin once said: "Those who would give up essential liberty to purchase a little temporary safety deserve neither liberty nor safety.[107]

Chapter 10

Fitting into the Picture

"It is necessary to the happiness of man that he be mentally faithful to himself. Infidelity does not consist in believing or disbelieving, it consists in professing to believe what he does not believe...[In doing so,] he has prepared himself for the commission of every other crime."

Thomas Paine

If you've read all of the previous material, you are probably wondering what, if anything, you can do to prevent the impending disaster from destroying this beautiful country. As the title of this chapter implies, you may have some adjusting to do to find where you fit in in the political spectrum that exists in America today.

There are four choices really: Democrat, Republican, Independent, and Libertarian. Several other parties exist, such as the Green Party, The US Marijuana Party, and, believe it or not, The Rent is 2 Damn High Party.[108] Hopefully, their organization and strength is such that they aren't really strong parties, and in spite of their "merits," they haven't caught the soul of Americans. There are other splinter groups of various kinds. It's up to you to determine where you really fit in or perhaps rather to find which fits you better.

It has been said that a young person who isn't a liberal has no heart and an older person who isn't a conservative has no head. When I was growing up, the Democratic Party had a strong hold on American politics. In a sense, it was heroic in stature, and most children who were being raised in large cities aspired to become a member of that party. I really cannot say what the status of the Democratic Party in rural communities was at that time. If it was comparable to what it is today, I would imagine that the Republican Party had a foothold in rural communities and smaller cities, but I didn't pay attention to this at the time. So it was with a sense of pride that I enrolled in the Democratic Party when I came of age in 1959 so that I was much pleased to be able to vote for John F. Kennedy. I continued to maintain my affiliation with the Democratic Party but I noticed as time progressed that most of the news reports about the Republican Party were negative in nature, implying that the Republican Party was partial to the wealthy and the Democratic Party represented the common person. This, of course, was an oversimplification.

When I finished graduate school, I moved to Massachusetts, which was the hotbed of Democratic thinking, negative news reports about the Republican Party continued unabated, but for some reason they became more and more unbelievable. As I continued to listen and to see the effects of the one-party state, I couldn't help but question my political affiliation.

I maintained my party membership but began to tell people that I remained a Democrat to prove that there was at least one Democrat in the state of Massachusetts who didn't have to go to a proctologist for a brain scan. I began to see that the people running for offices in Massachusetts that I thought were best qualified to serve in the various offices were almost always Republican. But most Republicans running for office were defeated. In spite of how much it seemed like swimming against the tide, I finally resolved to become a Republican.

Naturally, most of my Democrat friends treated me as if I had abandoned the true faith. But I began to see more and more clearly that the action I had taken, while futile, was the wisest thing I could have done. I haven't regretted it, and in the years since, I've seen that I had not left the Democratic Party; it had left me.

Allow me to explain. With age comes wisdom, and it's clear that the Democratic Party, especially in Massachusetts, is self-serving at best. If we examine the policies of the Democratic Party carefully, this begins to be apparent to even the staunchest defender of the Democratic philosophy; through either perfidy or naïveté, they refuse to acknowledge it. For example, most of the people crying for legitimacy for illegal aliens are Democrats, and what motivates the leaders is the hope that these illegals will become members of the Democratic Party and votes Democratic.

Most of the entitlement programs, perhaps almost all of them, are designed for the same reason: that these socialist programs will appeal to the beneficiaries, who will then cleave to the Democratic Party and vote the party line. I do not intend to imply that all of these programs are necessarily all bad, but it's clear that there is a hook buried in most of them and that many of them are interconnected.

For example, it seems clear that the current US administration has no intention of stopping illegal entry or even deporting illegal aliens who are caught by law enforcement for other infringements. This is evident in the lack of enforcement of border crossings through the tying of the hands of law enforcement in the border states and not constructing adequate fences to prevent illegal entry into this country. There seem to have been many illegal border crossings throughout the history of the Mexican-American interface, but it has progressed to the point that there are now millions of illegal aliens in the United States. The number who have been caught and should be deported has grown to the point that one or two daily airline flights would not be enough to contain the problem. Perhaps a fleet of troop ships could solve the problem?

Such issues have been dealt with more thoroughly in the preceding chapters, but it should be clear that those who choose to remain in the Democratic Party have their work cut out for them. Just as a three-party system will not work, neither will a one-party system—just as it has not worked in Massachusetts. That state's governor, Deval Patrick, a sycophant of the president, claims to espouse diversity, but clearly only if it doesn't entail a different party affiliation.

As it stands now, the Democratic Party is a major part of the problem that must be remedied for there to be any hope of a future in this country. Perhaps the answer is to reconstruct the Democratic Party along its original lines. To fail to do this will result in the eventual destruction of the two-party system. This, in turn, will result in a one-party system that will become the beginning of the end of America. Only with the two-party system can real, across-the-aisle cooperation result.

What You Can Do

Actions I have taken can be taken by anyone who has read this book. But don't act if you lack the full motivation to do so. It remains to be seen whether the Republicans have any better solution to our country's ailments. The plain truth is that no political party is anywhere close to perfect.

Although there are several choices available to all of you, it might be best that you spend your efforts at cleaning up the party to which you belong. However, this is a long-term process and is perhaps best begun after the immediate needs of our country are dealt with. Each of us needs to consider what we must do in the short term.

If you, as I, feel that our country is in immediate and clear danger and that if it is allowed to progress on its current course it will serve none of us, then it's time to decide what to do. Of one thing I'm certain: only through our determination to oversee all the activities of our representatives can we be sure that, whatever party is in office, its actions will be in the best interests of America.

And that can happen only by exercising our duty to make certain that the shenanigans of the past are kept in the past. We have to stop thinking that they will do what is best without our watching them and writing to them as often as possible. If we shirk this responsibility, we will have only ourselves to blame when America ends up in the trash bin of history. When that happens, we will all have to face our children and our grandchildren and say, "It was my laziness and lack of conscience that caused this. I am too ashamed to even beg for your forgiveness." For now, we have the following to consume our time and energy.

The Presidential Candidates

At the time of this writing, there are still three or possibly four or more candidates. The Democrats have clearly fielded Barack Obama, the incumbent who has led us into the mess we are in. His intent seems to be to pursue the same course over the next four years, particularly those activities in which he has had less than desired success. I believe that his intentions are to place the United States of America on a decidedly socialist footing and to surrender us to the supranational United Nations. We have seen how this can be done, and we must fight against it by writing to our senators and congresspeople, telling them that we are opposed to being a part of the United Nations.

The Republicans have three current candidates: Mitt Romney, Rick Santorum, and Newt Gingrich. Romney appears to be the current leader and the most electable of the three. However, anything can happen between now and the convention in August. The only thing we can do now is actively support whoever becomes the standard bearer of the Republican Party. We can't afford a debacle similar to Ross Perot's scuttling of the Republicans' chance of victory over the Democrats.

According to the latest polls, at the time of this writing, Romney seems to have the best chance of beating Obama. In an article in the March 12, 2012, issue of the *Weekly Standard*, [109] author Michael Warren suggested that Obama has a seven-point lead over Santorum, whereas Romney has a nine-point lead over Obama. Among college-educated voters, Romney has a sixteen-point lead whereas Obama has a twenty-four-point lead over Santorum. So, it seems that Romney has a better chance than Santorum. Polls are not elections, nor do they predict the results of Conventions. Support the Republican Party choice; steer clear of "wildcat" contenders. The choice of the Republican Party may not be yours under the best of circumstances, but no matter; support that candidate in every way, or risk the consequences. Stand up and be counted. Talk to your friends and ask them to support the person running against Obama. Make sure that you vote and that you help others who may be unable to reach the polls on their own. Be a good citizen voter and stand up for America. You can't blame anyone else if you fail to do your share of the job.

The Issues before America

To have read everything in this book means nothing if nothing is done to change the state of the country. Go back over the book with a marker, and highlight the issues discussed in each chapter. Take seriously the suggestion to write letters or e-mails to your representatives in Congress. If you don't press your case with your government representatives, little if anything can come of you having purchased and read this book.

The more that you practice communicating with your senators and representatives, the easier it becomes. The payback will take place when you see your representative voting as you have requested and perhaps even quoting your input to him or her. It's a small enough price to pay for good government. Congresspeople are easily enticed to act in way that harm this country when they believe no one is watching, or worse, that no one cares. Absent the assertions of one's constituents, the honest legislator may succomb to the many temptations that often assail them.

Get a Gun and Learn to Use It

By nature, I'm neither an alarmist nor a man of violence. But like most of you, I'm willing to defend my family and my country, even though I'm pretty much a useless old codger. God forbid that the bad scenarios I've pictured come to be. When your rights are lost or your family is threatened, whether by violent people or by a government gone amuck, you can't merely say, "Leave us alone!" You have to do something—that is, arm yourself.

However, if you get a gun, get a cool head along with it and a magazine filled with wisdom. There may be a terrific price to pay to retrieve the rights we share under our Constitution. Learn to shoot well and safely, and teach your loved ones to do so. You can't always be there to protect your family, so don't take a chance on leaving them unprotected. Owning a gun comes with grave responsibilities, so if you aren't going to learn how to use it wisely and teach your family to do likewise, you are better off not buying one.

The price you will pay is a great one if you fail to use your instincts and brain wisely. God willing, you will never use it in anger. The injury or death of a family member or an innocent bystander will leave you in deep remorse for the rest of your life.

Also join the National Rifle Association. In spite of casual and unfounded remarks to the contrary, you'll find that fine organization to be your first line of defense in both shooter education and the protection of your rights.

Finale

In spite of all of its faults, America is still the best place in the world to live. God blessed us with forefathers who knew what they were doing and who really worked to get it right. I like to believe that we will encounter them in the next life, and they will wonder how we protected what they had set aside for us.

Most of us had little to do with the many problems that have begun to infest our beautiful homeland. Perhaps we failed to open our mouths when we first saw something wrong. But one thing is certain: from today on, we have no excuse for failing to do so.

We have inherited the best place in the world in which to live, but it's not just a vacationland. We can look back and see that it was turned over in near-perfect condition. If we act correctly, we can begin the task of passing it on once again in the same near-perfect condition or better than when we received it.

America is currently in a state of crisis just as it was in 1775. I hope the ideas in this document are as pertinent as those in the original *Common Sense*.

"If there must be trouble, let it be in my day so my child may have peace."

Thomas Paine

Epilogue

"It is necessary to the happiness of man that he be mentally faithful to himself."

Thomas Paine

By now, you have no doubt realized the truth of the old adage "If it's important or must be done right, do it yourself!" To that end, in the appendix I have included a template for your letters and e-mails to your political representatives. If you truly want to see change, you must be prepared to write to them until it becomes almost habitual. If you don't do it, who will? Fortunately, we are only responsible for ourselves.

During the past several years, we've seen government intrusion and the cost of government increasing at an alarming rate. And we hear the often-repeated refrain "We inherited this from the previous administration." Of course, this is true of every administration; everyone inherits something, whether good or bad. Usually the good is not complained about and may even be passed off as originating with the current administration.

The bad, on the other hand, increases in its effect relative to anything good that may have happened in the previous four years. This is especially true of the current administration. Despite complaining about the fiscal policies of the Bush administration, the Obama administration has outdone them on all levels. There seems to be no amount of money or no cause unworthy of financing at the people's expense. Granted, Bush's fiscal policies may have also been inappropriate. But there is little or no excuse for compounding this by undertakings such as ObamaCare, government bailouts of private industry, raising the debt ceiling, the Solyndra scandal, and numerous other unwise and poorly considered programs.

Make no mistake about it; America is at a crossroads. We are a "house divided," and only a decidedly rightward change in direction will allow us to bring together the various groups within this country and put America on a new and true heading. Without such action—our action—America will continue to drift to the left on a course replete with unconscionable spending and greater and greater disregard for the Constitution that made this country what it is.

But this can't be done without your willingness. It's time for all Americans to jump party lines if necessary and vote for a Republican administration that, God willing, can pull us from this downward spiral.

Remember to watch whoever is elected carefully, watch whomever is assisting that person, and holler like an injured puppy whenever an attempt is made to either enlarge or fail to reduce the size of this bloated government wisely. Watch carefully and, if necessary, complain vigorously about government spending habits, so that we will not remain a spendthrift government.

In closing, let's invoke once more the words of Thomas Paine:

These are the times that try men's souls. The summer soldier and the sunshine patriot will, in this crisis, shrink from the service of their country; but he that stands it now, deserves the love and thanks of man and woman. Tyranny, like hell, (or like government let loose) is not easily conquered; yet we have this consolation with us, that the harder the conflict, the more glorious the triumph. What we obtain too cheap, we esteem too lightly: it is dearness only that gives everything its value.

Appendix

"We have it in our power to begin the world over again."

Thomas Paine

Date

The Honorable _____

US Senate

Washington, DC 20515

or The Honorable_____

US House of Representatives

Washington, DC 20510

Dear Senator_____:

or Dear Congressman _____:

or Dear Congresswoman _____:

I am writing to you to advise you of my feeling about the following:

....

I believe we should *(or should not)*...

I am your constituent and I am proud to say that I always vote.

Sincerely,

Resources

"The mind once enlightened cannot again become dark."

Thomas Paine

Steyn, Mark, *After America*. Washington, D.C.: Regnery Publishing, 2011.

Steyn, Mark, *America Alone*, Washington, D.C., Regnery Publishing, 2006.

LaPierre, Wayne, *America Disarmed*, Washington, D.C., WND Books, ISBN 978-1-936488-43-1, pp. 201-224

Schweizer, Peter, *Architects of Ruin*, New York, NY, Harper-Collins, 2011.

Isaacson, Walter, *Benjamin Franklin-An American Life*, New York, NY, Simon and Schuster, Inc., 2003.

Bell, Jeffrey, *The Case for Polarized Politics, Why America Needs Social Conservatism*, New York, NY, Encounter Books, 2012.

Malkin, Michelle, *Culture of Corruption: Obama and his Team of Tax Cheats, Crooks and Cronies*, Washington, D.C., Regnery Publishing, 2010.

Beck, Glen, *Glen Beck's Common Sense*, Simon and Schuster, Inc., NewYork, NY, 2009.

McCarthy, Andrew C., *The Grand Jihad*, New York, NY, Encounter Books, 2010.

Balkin, Jack M., *Living Originalism*, Belknap Press, Cambridge, MA, 2011.

Skousen, Mark, *The Making of Modern Economics*, 2nd *Ed.*, M.E. Sharpe, Armonk, NY, 2009, ISBN 978-0-7656-2226-3

Lott, Jr., John R., *More Guns, Less Crime*, Univ. of Chicago Press, Chicago, IL, 1998

Shirer, William L., *The Rise and Fall of the Third Reich*, Simon and Schuster, New York, NY, 1960.

Fonte, John, *Sovereignty or Submission*, Encounter Books, New York, NY, 2011.

Endnotes

1   Thomas Paine, *Common Sense* (New York: Fall River Press, 1995), p. xv

2   Walter Isaacson, *Benjamin Franklin-An American Life*, (New York, Simon & Schuster, 2003), page 459

3   *Ida D. Brudnick, Congressional Salaries and Allowances, Congressional Research Service, 7-5700, Jan 4, 2012, p.9-12, see: www.crs.gov*

4   Michael D. Tanner, *"Bad Medicine – a Guide to the Real Costs and Consequences of the New Health Care Law"*, Cato Institute, Washington, 2011 pp. 25-33, See also: *http://www.cato.org/bad-medicine* Accessed 2/1/12

5   Robert Pear, *"Insider Trading Ban for Lawmakers Clears Congress"*, New York Times, 3/22/12, *http://www.nytimes.com/2012 /03/22/us/politics/insider-trading-ban-for lawmakers clears,* Accessed 5/9/12

6   George W. Mixter, *Primer of Navigation, 2nd Ed., ,* (New York,Van Nostrand, 1943), pp. 22-62, 251ff., 279

7   Mark Steyn, *America Alone, ,* (Washington, Regnery Publishing Co., 2011), p. xvii

8   William Morris, Ed., *American Heritage Dictionary, (Boston,* Houghton Mifflin Co., ISBN 0-395-20360-0, 1980)

9   Monica Davey, *"Blagojevich Sentenced to 14 Years in Prison",* The New York Times, Dec., 7, 2011, or: http://www.nytimes. com-/2011/12/08/us/blagojevich-expresses-remorse-in-courtroom-speech.html

10 Kevin D. Williamson, *Repo Men,* National Review, Dec. 19, 2011, p.39

11 Williamson, Ibid., p. 40

12 Peter Schweizer, *Throw Them All Out: How Politicians and Their Friends Get Rich Off Insider Stock Tips, Land Deals, and Cronyism That Would Send The Rest of Us to Prison,* (New York, Houghton Mifflin Harcourt Trade, 1980)

13 Tom Fitton, *"The Verdict,"* The Judicial Watch, February 2012, 425Third St., SW, Suite 800, Washington, DC, 20024, or: *www. judicialwatch.org/*

14 If you want a copy of this issue of *The Verdict,* please write to: Editor, The Judicial Watch Verdict, 425 Third St., SW, Suite 800, Washington, DC 20024 and ask for Vol. 18,

Issue #2. I do not know the single issue cost but an annual subscription, including membership, is $35.00.

15 Brett Decker, "Clean Green fraud," The Washington Times National Weekly, Editorial, Feb. 13, 2012, p. 38

16 Author(s) unknown, " ATF's Fast and Furious scandal", http://www.latimes.com/news/nationworld/nation/atf-fast-furious-sg,0,3828090.storygallery. Accessed 5/13/12.

17 Wayne LaPierre, America Disarmed, (Washington, WND Books, 2011), pp.208-224.

18 Diana West, "Washington Seals Records that Might Embarrass Insiders", The Washington Examiner, 12/10/2011, The Judicial Watch, Vol. 18, #2, p. 18.

19 Thomas Fitton, 'Judicial Watch Releases List of Washington's Top "Ten Most Wanted" Corrupt Politicains for 2011, The Judicial Watch, Vol. 18, #2, p. 1, 2/12. ."The Judicial Watch noted, "That's about as secret as it gets."

20 Emily Miller, "Tax cheats on the federal rolls", Washington Times, 1/25/12, http://www.washingtontimes.com/news /2012/jan/25/tax-cheats-on-the-federal-rolls/, Accessed 2/22/12

21 "Solyndra scandal exposes the lie of governmnent 'investment'", 9/2011, The Washington Examiner, http://washington examiner.com/2011/09/solyndra-scandal-exposes-lie-government...,

Accessed 3/12/12., See also: *http://online.wsj.com/article/ B10001424053111904836...*

22 Gordon Tullock, *"Government Spending"*, Library of Economics and Liberty, *http//www.econlib.org/library/enc1/ governmentspending.html*, Accessed 2/3/12.

23 *http//www.usgovernmentspending.com/*

24 Supporting Graphs from Library of Economics and Liberty, See Ref. 22,*http://www.econlib.org/library/enc1/art/fig06.jpg*, Accessed 2/3/12.

25 Mark Skousen, *The Making of Modern Economics*, 2nd Ed., *(Armonk*, M.E. Sharpe, 2009), p. 111.

26 *"Executive Order – National Commission of Fiscal Responsibility and Reform,"* White House Office of the Press Secretary, Feb., 18, 2010.

27 James Pethokoukis, *"A Tax Floor with no Ceiling,"* National Review, Feb. 20, 2012, p 16

28 Richard W. Rahn, *"Government spending jobs myth,",* The Washington Times, Dec. 26, 2011, p. 32

29 Christopher Chantrill, Compiler, *"US Defense Spending History, http//www.usgovernmentspending.com/defense_ spending, Accessed 2/8/12.*

30 Christopher Chantrill, Compiler, *"US Defense Spending History"*, *http://www.usgovernmentdebt.us/defense_spending*, Accessed 2/8/12.

31 James Gattuso and Diane Katz, *"Red Tape Rising – A 2011 Mid-Year Report"*, The Heritage Foundation, 7/25/11, *http// www.heritage.org/research/reports/2011/07/red-tape-rising-a-2011-midyear-report,*Accessed 2/3/12.

32 Council of Economic Advisors, *"Economic Report of the President"*, *Table B-80, February 2011, http://www.gpoaccess.gov /eop/2011/pdf/ERP-2011.pdf*, Accessed 2/3/12.

33 James Gattuso, et al.,*"Red Tape Rising: Obama's Torrent of New Regulation"*, Heritage Foundation Backgrounder #2482, Oct. 26,2010, *http://www.heritage.org/Research /reports/2010/10/red-tape-rising-obamas-torrent-of-new-regulation*, Accessed 2/3/12.

34 Thomas Sowell Quotes, 9/21/11, *http://redwhitebluenews.com /?page_id=24605, Accessed on 3/10/12.*

35 *Investor's Business Daily, quoted in Liberty Guard Publication No. LIB-033-IN, P.O. Box 96292, Washington, DC 20090-6292.*

36 Iain Murray, "Leviathan", *National Review Online, Feb 3, 2011, Acessed on 2/26/12 on: http//www.nationalreview.com/ articles/258768/leviathan -iain-murray, Accessed on 2/26/12*

37 *Investor's Business Daily, ibid.*

38   *The Wall Street Journal,* as quoted by Liberty Guard Communication No. LIB-033-BILL, P.O. Box 96292, Washington, DC 20090-6292; See also: Elizabeth MacDonald, *"Government Workers earn More Than their Private-Sector Count-erparts",* 1/31/12 Fox Business, <u>*http://www.foxbusiness. com/*</u> *politics/2012/01/31/government-workers-earns-more-than-pri*...Accessed 5/11/12. See also: Stephen Dinan, *"CBO says federal workers rake in much more pay",* Washington Times Weekly Edition, 2/6/12.

39   Paul C. Light, Prof., *"The New True Size of Government",* Research Brief #2, Wagner Graduate School, New York University, August, 2006, Accessed 5/9/12.

40   Rep. Jason Chaffetz (R-UT), HR2560, *Cut, Cap & Balance Act of 2011,* 7/15/11,<u>www.govtrack.us/congress/bills /112/hr2560, Accessed on 3/10/12.</u>

41   If you wish additional information about this bill (HR 2560), please write to Liberty Guard, P.O. Box 96292, Washington, DC 20090-6292, or write to your Senator or Congressperson.

42   *The Wall Street Journal,* as quoted by Liberty Guard Communication No. LIB-033-BILL, P.O. Box 96292, Washington, DC 20090-6292.

43   Stephen Dinan *"Social Security reserves forecast to run dry by 2022,"* The Washington Times Weekly Edition, February 20, 2012, p. 3.

44   Tiffany N. Anthony, *"Young Americans for Social Security Reform, 1/18/2005, http://www.stopstealingourmoney.blogspot.com* Accessed 5/12/12. See also: Allen W. Smith, Ph.D., *"Economist says Social Security in Trouble by 2018", 1/24/05, http://Archive.newsmax.com/archives/articles/2005/1/23/194653.shtml.* Accessed 5/12/12

45   Peter Ferrara, "Awinning Plan for Social Security Reform", Forbes, 3/17/11, Available on: *http//www.forbes.com/sites/peterferrara/2011/03/17a-winning-plan-for-social-security reform.html,* Accessed on 2/4/12.

46   Michael D. Tanner, "The 6.2 Percent Solution: A Plan for reforming Social Security", Cato Institute, 2/17/04, *http//www.cato.org/pub_display.php?pub_id=1618* Accessed on 2/4/12.

47   Brookings Events, "Saving Social Security: Which Way to Reform?", 12/10/03, Available on:*http//www.brookings.edu / events/2003/1210community-development.aspx* Accessed on 2/4/12.

48   Peter A. Diamond and Peter R. Orszag, "Reforming Social Security: A Balanced Plan", Brookings Institution 12/03,

http//www.brookings.edu/papers/2003/12saving_orszag.aspx Accessed on 2/4/12.

49 .Geoffrey Kollman and Dawn Nuschler, *"Social Security Reform"*, *Congressional Research Service, 10/8/02 http//www. policyalmanac.org/social_welfare/archive/crs_social_security_ reform.hstml,* Accessed on 2/4/12

50 Gene Sperling, *"A Progressive Framework for Social Security Reform,"* Center for American Progress, *www.americanprogress. org*

51 Peter Schweitzer, *Architects of Ruin, (New York, ,* Harper-Collins, 2010), pp. 46-76.

52 Special Report #67, *"Obama to Spend 10.3 Trillion on Welfare: Uncovering the Full Cost of Means-Tested Welfare or Aid to the Poor"*, The Heritage Foundation, 9/16/09 *http://www.heritage. org research/reports/2009/09/Obama-to-spend-103-trillion-on-wefare....* Accessed on 1/31/12

53 Robert Rector and Kirk Johnson, Ph.D., *"Understanding Poverty in America"*, The Heritage Foundation, 1/5/04, *http:// www.heritage.org/research/reports/2004/01/under-standing-poverty-in-america* Accessed 2/1/12.

54 *ABC World News with Diane Sawyer, Friday Mar. 2, 2012*

55 Brooks Jackson, *"Newt's Faulty Food Stamp Claim"*, 1/18/12, updated 2/5/12, *http://www.Factcheck.org/2012/01/newts-faulty-food-stamp-claim/, Accessed 5/11/12.*

56 *National Committee Against the U.N. Takeover*, a Special Project of America's Survival, Inc., P.O. Box 96099, Washington, D.C. 20090-6099

57 *Communication from U.S. Freedom Fund, P.O. Box 96601, Washington DC,20090, Freedom Fund is an authorized program of the Civic Council, a 501c(4) organization.*

58 Rep. Ron Paul, M.D., *"HR1146: American Sovreignty Act of 2009"*, 7/29/03, *http//www.govtrack.us/congress/bills /112/ hr1146*, Accessed 2/3/12.

59 Paul Bedard, *"Democrats Oppose Obama-U.N. Gun Control Treaty"*, USNews.com, 7/26/11, *http://www.usnews.com/ news /blogs/washington-whispers/2011/07/26/democrats-oppose-obama...*, See Also: Cliff Kincaid, *"Obama's Ambitious U.N.Treaty Agenda"* Accuracy in Media, 7/8/09, *http://www. aim.org/aim-column/obamas-ambitious-u-u-treaty-agenda/* , See also: Joseph Abrams, *"Boxer Seeks to Ratify U.N. Treaty That May Erode U.S. Rights"*,Fox News.com, 2/25/09, *http:// www.foxnews.com /politics/2009/02/25/boxer-seeks-ratify-treaty-erode-rights/*, See also: Cliff Kincaid, *"Obama Goal of International Law and U.N. Treaties Fails – Barely"*,

USNews, 7/11/11, *http://www.boogai.net/us-news/obama-goal-of-international-law-and-u-n-treaties-fails-barely/* Accessed 5/13/12

60 *Communication from Freedom Alliance, P.O. Box 97242, Washington DC 20090*

61 *Americans for Sovereignty, P.O. Box 96061, Washington, DC 20090-6091. Americans for Sovereignty is a project of Council for America, a 501c(4) organization.*

62 *Isaacson, Ibid. , page 313*

63 Author(s) unknown, *"Immigration to the United States"*, no date,*http//en.wikipedia.org/wiki/Immigration_to_the_United_States*, Accessed 2/23/12.

64 Author(s) unknown, "Requirements for applying for Citizenship in the United States", Harrington Law Offices, (no date), *http//immigration.findlaw.com/citizenship/ requirements -for-applying-for-citizenship-in-the-United-States.,* Accessed 2/23/12.

65 Multiple authors, *Official English Factsheets: Costs of Multilingualism"*, U.S.English, *http://www.usenglish.org/ view/301* See also: Natalia J. Garland, *"Languages in America: Legislation and Costs"*, *http://totalsurfer.bizland.com/topics_159*

.html See also: www.proenglish.org, *P. O. Box 97005, Washington, DC 20090-7005*

66 Bill Korach, *"Omar Ahmad Co-Founder of Cair: Islam in America Must Become Dominant Faith"*, 1/17/12,*http://education-curriculum-reform-government-schools.org/w/2012/01omar-ahmad-co-founder...*, Accessed 5/12/12.

67 Author(s) unknown, *"Illegal Immigration to the United States"*, *No date., http//en.wikipedia.org/wiki/Illegal_immigration _to_ the-_United_States*, Accessed 2/23/12.

68 P.F.Wagner and Dan Amato, *"The Dark Side of Illegal Immigration"*, *Digger's Realm*, *undated*, *http://www. usillegalaliens .com/impacts_of_illegal_immigration_diseases. html*, Accessed 5/12/12.

69 Author(s) unknown, *"Illegal Immigration Statistics"*, *undated, http//www.illegalimmigrationstatistics.org/*. Accessed 5/12/12.

70 Denise A. Vanison, et al., *"Administrative Alternatives to Comprehensive Immigration Reform"*, US-CIS, undated draft, *www.cis.gov*, Accessed 5/13/12, See also: *World Net Daily, as quoted by The Conservative Caucus, 2012*

71 *http//www.illegalimmigrationstatistics.org/, ibid.*

72 Mathew Boyle, *"Unions Fuel Democratic Party Financially"* The Daily Caller, February 19, 2011,*http://dailycaller.com*

/2011/02/19/*unions-fuel-democratic-party-financially*, Accessed 3/1/12.

73   Author(s) unknown, *"Barack Obama: Community Organizer"*, 4/21/08, *http//riverdaughter.wordpress.com/2008/04/21obama-the-community-organizer/*, Accessed 3/1/12

74   Stanley Kurtz, *"Inside Obama's Acorn"*, National Review Online, May 29, 2008, as reported in *http//www.nationalre view.com/articles/224610/inside-obamas-acorn/Stanley-kurtz* Accessed on 3/1/12.

75   Sol Stern, *"ACORN's Nutty Regime for Cities"*, City Journal, Spring 2003 as reported in *http//www.cityjournal.org/ html/13_2_acorns_nutty_regime.html* Accessed on 3/2/12.

76   Dave Kopel, *"Holder Must Go"*, NRA Institute for Legislative Action, *http//www.nraila.org/news-issues/articles/2012 holder-must-go.aspx?s=&st=&ps=* ...,Accessed on 3/9/12.

77   Committee for Justice, A Constitutional Law Center, P.O. Box 96740, Washington, DC 20090-6740

78   Andrea Lafferty, Congressional Briefing Summary, Traditional Values Coalition, 2012, pp. 1-6,

79   If you have not received any information relative to this task force, contact the Traditional Values Coalition and request the Task Force Supporter Response form or write to your

representatives, as well as to Chief Justice John Roberts and demand that Justice Kagan either recuse herself or be impeached.

80   Sol Sanders, "Follow the Money: High potential packed into a pipeline", Washington Times Weekly Edition, 12/26/11. See also: Kevin D. Williamson, *"The Truth about Fracking,"* National Review, February 20, 2012, p. 26   See also: Rich Trzupek, *"The age of environmental fear,"* Washington Times National Weekly, Jan, 30, 2012, p. 29

81   Kevin D. Williamson, *"The Central Plan,"* National Review, March 5, 2012, p 22.

82   Ben Wolfgang, *"Fracking firm calls EPA move a threat to whole industry,"* The Washington Times National Weekly, Dec. 26, 2011, p.11, See also Abby Schachter, *"Energy Independence and Its Enemies",* Commentary, June 2012, pp. 24-29.

83   Author(s) unknown, *"EPA classifies milk as oil, forcing costly rules on farmers"* Mlive, 6/14/10, *http://search.mlive.com/ EPA+milk+is+an+oil.* Accessed 3/2/12

84   Dave Boyer with Susan Crabtree, *"Obama offers $3.8 Trillion spending Plan,"* The Washington Times, Monday, Feb. 20, 2012. P. 7

85   Russell Gold, *"Faulty Wells, Not Fracking, Blamed for Water Pollution,"* The Wall Street Journal, Mar 13, 2012., p.1

86 http://www.cato.org/bad-medicine, ibid.

87 Dave Boyer with Susan Crabtree, *"Obama offers $3.8 Trillion spending Plan,"* The Washington Times, Monday, Feb. 20, 2012, p. 6

88 Ibid.

89 William L. Shirer, *The Rise and Fall of the Third Reich*, (New York Simon & Schuster, 1960), page 5.

90 Joseph Farah, *"Obama's militarization of the homefront,"* Creator s.Com, Undated, *http://www.creators.com/conservative /joseph-farah/obama-s-militarization-of-the-homefront*, Accessed 5/14/12.

91 Chris Cox, *"Holder tells Congress the Obama Administration wants to ban guns"*, NRA Institute for Legislative Action, 2/8/12, *http://dailycaller.com/2012/02/08holder-tells-congress-the-obama-administration-wants-to-ban-guns* Accessed on 3/9/12

92 Paul Gallant *et al.*, *"The Arms Trade Treaty and our Constitution's Loophole"*, 2/27/12, http//www.ammoland.com/2012/02/27/ the-arms-trade-treaty-our-constitutions-loophole, Accessed 3/9/12.

93 John R. Lott, Jr., *More Guns, Less Crime*, (Chicago, Univ. of Chicago Press, 1998), Chaps. 3-4.

94 Chris Cox, *"Obama: Anti-gun Arrogance vs. the Constitution"*, NRA Institute for Legisative Action, 2/20/12 *http://nraila.org/news-issues/articles/2012/Obama-anti-gun-arrogance-vs-the-constitution.aspx* Accessed on 3/9/12

95 *Gallant, op. cit., p. 4.*

96 Joseph Bruce Alonso, *"The Second Amendment and Global Gun Control"*, Journal on Firearms & Public Policy, Vol. 15, pp.1-35, (2002)

97 David Koppel, et. al., *"The Human Right of Self-Defense,"* Brigham Young University Journal of Public Law, Vol. 22, Number 1, (pp.56-57)

98 Dave Boyer, *"GOP fears Obama will sell out to Russia,"* The Washington Times Weekly Edition, Monday, April 2, 2012, p. 3

99 Boyer, Ibid.

100 Frank L. Gaffney, Jr., *"Leading no followers and wrecking the U.S. deterrent,"* The Washington Times Weekly Edition, Monday, April 2, 2012, p. 31

101 Declan McCullagh, "National ID Cards on the way", Available also on *http://news.cnet.com/National-ID-cards-on-the-way/2100-1028_3-5573414.html Accessed on 3/12/12.*

102 "A national ID card for American citizens?", _http://_
endoftheamericandream.com/archives/a-national-id-card-for-
american-citizens-get-r....Accessed on 3/12/12

103 _Ezra Klein, "Is a biometric national ID card an immigration_
game-changer?" Also _http://voices.washingtonpost.com/ezraklein/_
_2010/04/is_a_biometric_national-_id_car.html..._

104 Chris Cox, _"Obama: Anti-Gun Arrogance vs. the Constitution"_
NRA Institute for Legislative Action, 2/20/12 _http://nraila._
org/news-issues/articles/2012/Obama-anti-gun-arrogance-vs-the-
constitution.aspx. Accessed 3/9/12

105 Joseph Farah, _ibid._

106 "NDAA Bill allows military to indefinitely detain American
citizens without due process" , Also available on http://
thesteadydrip.blogspot.com/2011/12/ndaa-bill-allows-
military-to.html Accessed on 3/13/12.

107 Quotations of Benjamin Franklin, inter alii. _http://www._
quotationspage.com/quote/1381.html

108 Patrick Hruby, "Beyond duopoly, Third parties are the ideal
lab of American politics", Washington Times Weekly Edition,
3/12/12.

109 Michael Warren, _"Who Can Beat Obama?"_ The Weekly
Standard, March 12, 2012, p. 13

Index

Index